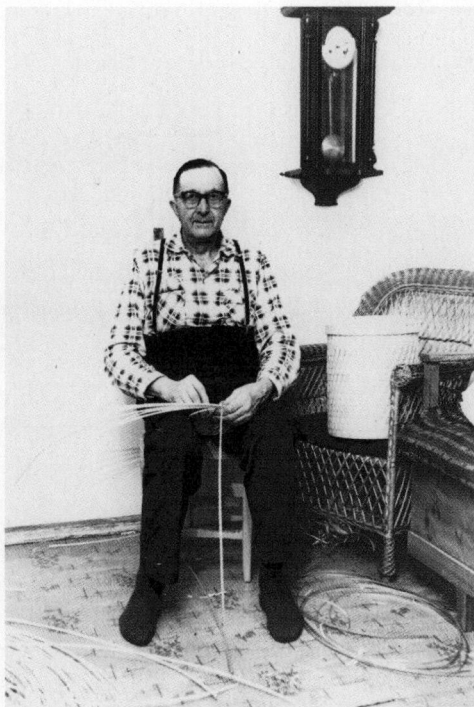

To Lennart

THE LAST
BASKET MAKER
AND I

THE COMPLETION OF THIS PROJECT has been a long time coming. The making of this book has stretched across a period where I have, through, and alongside the research, both grown as a person and practitioner. I have further come into my own. I often think of this book as my own coming-of-age story—a great contemplation of one's belonging in the world—broken down into various facets of exploration.

During the process of putting together the body of work that these texts would become a part of, I have been exposed to a diverse range of knowledge when collaborating with people who each hold their own well of specialised expertise. Through these interactions, I have been able to hone in on a range of specific areas of interest, and have been introduced to new methods of research collection, writing, and making. Learning how to comprehend and put these methods into practice is a process which (like most learning processes) has been far from linear. I started this project upon completing my undergraduate degree in textile design, and in its infancy, some of the texts naturally adhered to an academic structure, reflecting their intended purpose of being evaluated and marked.

The original text, my then dissertation, had the title: 'From handmade to man-made and beyond: the handicraft evolution of the Hedared basket—*from essential necessity to decorative object*'.

Looking back, the project had, from the beginning, multiple objectives due to the layered nature of my interest in the Hedared basket. There were many aspects of the basket I wanted to explore and lots of perspectives I wanted to tie together. The unknown dimensions of all these layers quickly became an apparent feature of the research. It has taken time to devise the different methods of approaching, collecting and analysing the research. It has taken time for the reasoning behind including certain areas to become apparent, for the *why* to be fully formulated and put into words. Early on, I knew that my reasons for wanting to develop this body of work stretched beyond a mere desire to look at the basket from a 'design perspective' or to examine it from a place of reverence for cultural

3

history. With time, it became clear that these layered dimensions stemmed from a need to express my own lived experience by examining the basket and, by extension, the life of my great-grandfather Lennart.

Yet, before such time had passed, before this clarity of purpose had made itself known, before I had comprehended the connections between all these moving parts, the dissertation had the following section in its introduction:

> I will present the history of handicrafts in my
> home region of the Seven Districts and explore
> its future legacy of making. I will discuss how a
> contemporary design researcher combines tradi-
> tional crafts with theory when reflecting on new,
> relevant and sustainable making processes—
> I aim to explore how the cultural-historical her-
> itage of the Hedared basket can enrich the very
> notion of a design practice, reinforce a symbiotic
> relationship with nature, and affirm the sense of
> self for its practitioner. This text will approach
> these topics from a factual and evidence-based
> gaze, informed and fuelled by my personal and
> emotional investment in the basket, hopefully
> providing the 'big picture'.

Since then, my core areas of interest have indeed emerged more purposefully. This is reflected in the documentation. The project has moved away from wanting to be strictly academic. It has become more subjective, combining my own reflections with those of others, to complement this 'big picture'. Looking back at the initial text, I can decipher the outlines of my true reasons for exploring the basket, before I had found the words to articulate them. The true purpose and *felt* importance of my research only became apparent through the long process of collaboration and experimentation, as I encountered new people, methods, and ideas.

Throughout, I have strived to decipher tradition through its most dominant traits found in my primary culture:

4

the Swedish. I have sought to keep its values, customs and points of view intact as it filters through a new type of lived experience: my own. The majority of my family belongs to only one culture. I, as the son of a Swedish mother and a Tunisian father, alongside my queer identity, have a contrasting outlook on tradition and its accompanied principles. I have multiple cultural perspectives that influence my view of the world. Naturally, I seek to communicate these perspectives that, in contrast to my family, embody a new type of reality. I have sought to use craft as a means of positioning my own lived experience in relation to my great-grandfather's—to mirror his life and craft practice with my own.

Through our very different lived realities (both shaped by the presence of craft), the Hedared basket has helped to tease out the unknown, overlooked, or unacknowledged parts of the social and cultural evolution that has occurred between our generations. The many stories of the basket have helped to make sense of the relational ties between past and present.

The making of this patchwork is reflected in the writing: the tone, feel, and overall reading experience will noticeably fluctuate in narration and style. Each text reflects the particular moment in time at which it was written, whether it relays historical events, narrates pivotal moments of discovery, or just simply describes a thought process for my own making. My approach has been to embrace this plethora of ideas, impressions, and intentions. I wanted to capture the journey: one of learning, comprehending, and ultimately making—placing storytelling at the centre of my craft practice. I have kept Lennart in the rearview mirror. His influence continues to guide and anchor the work.

Hedared is a small village in the woods of west Sweden,
home to a socio-geographically unique basketry practice.
Its handicraft heritage forms the basis of this series of texts.
My Swedish great-grandfather Lennart Pettersson (1901–1985)
was born into a family of impoverished farmers in Hedared,
not far from where he later lived and worked, in the rural community of Risa. Hedared lies in the district of Veden,
one of seven that make up the *Sjuhärad* region. The Seven
Districts had been an epicentre of handicrafts since the Middle
Ages, and eventually a cottage industry developed around
its local practices. The then-closer proximity of Sjuhärad to
neighbouring Scandinavian countries (the Swedish borders
have since expanded) allowed prosperous trade routes to form.
This enhanced the reputation of the skilled craftsmen in the
Seven Districts, both in Sweden and internationally.[1] The historical cottage industry in the districts was domestically both
the oldest and most impactful.[2]

The Seven Districts: Bollebygd, Gäsene, Kind, Mark,
Redväg, Veden, and Ås, each had their own specialised practices. Examples include the predominance of weaving in Kind,
linen cultivation in the Mark district and woodworking in
Bollebygd.[3] The inhabitants were described by historian Nils
Hufwedsson Dal in the early 1700s as having used handicrafts
in trade since 'lawless and ancient times'.[4]

Borås is the capital city of Sjuhärad, founded in 1621.[5]
It is located about fifteen kilometres from Hedared, both are
found in the district of Veden. Historically, Veden was the
lesser-known district of Sjuhärad, with less defined borders than its neighbours. Named 'the district of the forest'
by former governor Bengt K.Å. Johansson, the landscape of
Veden consisted mostly of dense forests with fir and pine and
little agricultural land.[6] On older maps, the area is depicted
as largely unpopulated and uncultivated. It was not until the
nineteenth century when Sweden's population boomed,
that Veden saw greater agricultural development.[7] Although
blessed with an abundance of dense woods, the soil in

6

Veden's district has always been thin and far from plentiful. The majority of its farmers were thus unable to successfully and reliably cultivate their land, leading them to seek alternative forms of income—predominantly handcrafting objects of utility to trade. The villagers of Hedared were part of the rich cottage industry in the Seven Districts, trading their hand-crafted basketry to provide income. My great-grandfather Lennart Pettersson's practice exemplifies this fact.
He was taught the handicraft of basketry through an inter-generational exchange to help his family get by. From a young age, children of skilled artisans in the Seven Districts would assist the adults of the household in making goods to be traded.

In the late 1970s, large-scale basket making seemed a distant relic. It was during this time that the local craft association produced the documentary *Basketry in Hedared* (1978) as an attempt to preserve the handicraft. Solely dedicated to the making process of the Hedared basket, the film depicts a 77-year-old Lennart, leading the making alongside two apprentices. Together, they display the unique material process that makes the basket, capturing every nuance and property of the wood used. The film describes how artisans like Lennart, in order to procure its material, needed to familiarise themselves with their surroundings.[8] Such knowledge and understanding of the forest were essential, helping impoverished villagers to survive up until the first part of the twentieth century.

The documentary highlights how, eventually, Lennart became the sole active maker with this knowledge—the bearer of a cultural-historical legacy and the living embodiment of the historical skillfulness found in the Seven Districts. He was 'the last basket maker from Risa'.

This project is a patchwork, consisting of various moving parts that have come together to form a whole. I studied textile design, developing a close connection to craft-based making methods through my specialisation in handweaving. Due to the course's focus on design, my classmates and I were (broadly) taught how to situate this practice in an industrial context. One was often challenged to devise approaches to industrial conundrums and regularly invited by tutors to question standardised making processes deemed unsustainable due to environmental reasons. Students on the course were encouraged to approach such issues holistically, using their own field within textiles (which in my case was the medium of weaving) as a tool to do so.

Being a queer person with roots in both Sweden and Tunisia, I naturally have an extensive view of the world, anchored in the belief that inclusivity and representation matter, especially when it comes to issues of unsustainable development.

In the role of craft practitioner, as keeper of these multiple points of cultural reference, I am naturally intrigued by identity and finding that certain place of longing through my work. My mixed cultural heritage has instilled in me a need to explore the roles that place and social belonging play in storytelling, to anchor a body of work through a narrative, and redefine its given purpose—use storytelling as a tool to connect with the felt tensions between my cultures and process my own experiences of being othered.

This *felt* need assembles the process of weaving to become a freeing space in itself: a myriad of expressions where these multiple cultural identities can each find solace, coexist, and belong. Born in the early 1990s, I am a digital native. I was brought up with easy access to information alongside easy opportunities to connect with others via online spaces.

Such possibilities turn the internal (and often lonesome) contemplation of one's true place of belonging into a shared, collective experience. From a design perspective, contemplating the shared realities that others of my cultural background are conditioned to navigate while challenged to devise approaches to unsustainable industrial practices, translates into an effort to investigate making processes that interlink environmental issues with social or political inclusion—reflecting one's own relationality with the outside world.

Exploring such a process is at the heart of this project, one that encompasses the *felt* importance stemming from the said factors: a making process derived from a necessary plurality of approaches, leading to the recurring mention of this project as a patchwork becoming prevalent, again and again.

FADHEL AND LENNART

These twin realities: my great-grandfather's embodied skills as a means of survival, and my own sense of being in between cultural identities, have become the central narrative of the research. The story of the Hedared basket—its cultural-historical significance, social influence, and contemporary relevance has formed a mode of practice that in its extension has been an attempt to deconstruct the interconnections between our two realities—a detangling of the cultural elements and societal norms that have ultimately conditioned our relationship to making.

NOTES

1. Hufwedsson Dal, N. (1719) *Boërosia*, cited in Moritz, M. (1917) *Sveriges Officiella Statistik. Socialstatistik: Svensk hemindustri—Del II: Monografier*. Stockholm: Isaac Marcus' Boktryckeri-Aktiebolag, p. 9.
2. Moritz, M. (1917) 'Hemindustrin i södra Älvsborgs län'. In: *Sveriges Officiella Statistik. Socialstatistik: Svensk hemindustri—Del II: Monografier*. Stockholm: Isaac Marcus' Boktryckeri-Aktiebolag, p. 9.
3. Moritz, M. (1917) 'Hemindustrin i södra Älvsborgs län—Historiska notiser: 1. Gårdfarihandel och hemindustri'. In: *Sveriges Officiella Statistik. Socialstatistik: Svensk hemindustri—Del II: Monografier*. Stockholm: Isaac Marcus' Boktryckeri-Aktiebolag, pp. 9–10.
4. Hufwedsson Dal, N. (1719) *Boërosia*, quoted in Moritz, M. (1917) *Sveriges Officiella Statistik. Socialstatistik: Svensk hemindustri—Del II: Monografier*. Stockholm: Isaac Marcus' Boktryckeri-Aktiebolag, p. 9.
5. Andersson Palm, L. (2005) *Borås stads historia I: stad och omland fram till 1800-talets mitt*. Lund: Historiska Media, p. 31.
6. Johansson, B.K.Å. (1996) 'Inledning'. In: Wiklund, N. (Ed.), *Fässingen—Från Borås och de sju häraderna: Tema Vedens Härad*. Borås: Kulturhistoriska Föreningen, p. 9.
7. Ibid.
8. Jansson, I. (1978) *Slöjd från Sjuhärad: Korgslöjd i Hedared*. Borås: De sju häradernas hemslöjdsförening/Slöjd i Väst/Kulturförvaltningen VGR.

IMAGE CREDITS

Unless specified, all images were taken by the author in 2018 or 2020, or sourced from the author's personal photo albums. In the latter case, the dates and the photographer's identity are unknown.

Previous page: p. 1, Lennart Pettersson (1978). Photo: Kulturförvaltningen VGR.

Upcoming pages: pp. 11–16 (From the top left):
1. Aerial image of Hedared (1951). Photo: AB Flygtrafik/Vänersborgs museum.
2. Film still 1: Lenk, T. (1923) *Korgmakeri: Upptagen i Hedared, Älvsborgs län*. Stockholm: SF.
3. Film still 2: Lenk, T. (1923) *Korgmakeri: Upptagen i Hedared, Älvsborgs län*. Stockholm: SF.

11. Film still 3: Jansson, I. (1978) *Slöjd från Sjuhärad: Korgslöjd i Hedared*. Borås: De sju häradernas hemslöjdsförening/Slöjd i Väst/Kulturförvaltningen VGR.
12. Film still 4: Jansson, I. (1978) *Slöjd från Sjuhärad: Korgslöjd i Hedared*. Borås: De sju häradernas hemslöjdsförening/Slöjd i Väst/Kulturförvaltningen VGR.
13. Film still 5: Jansson, I. (1978) *Slöjd från Sjuhärad: Korgslöjd i Hedared*. Borås: De sju häradernas hemslöjdsförening/Slöjd i Väst/Kulturförvaltningen VGR.

26. *Still life* (2021). Photo: Molly Overstall Khan.
27. Weaving in progress (2023). Photo: Molly Overstall Khan.
28. Weaving in progress (2023). Photo: Molly Overstall Khan.
29. *Från Ovan* (2023). Photo: Alexis Rodríguez Cancino.
30. *Portrait of process* (2021). Photo: Molly Overstall Khan.

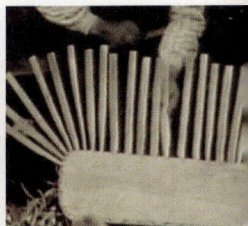

Innehåller ditt
RÖSTKORT
till valen den 9 september 2018

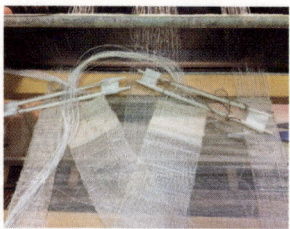

14

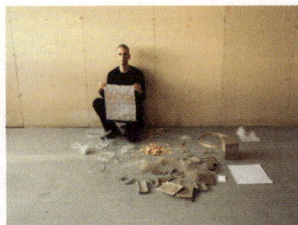

16

*PERSONAL
NOTES
ON BELONGING*

I FIND IT DIFFICULT TO ARTICULATE the frustration of not being perceived by one's peers as the rightful owner of our shared culture—despite all that I am, know, and do, to never be fully seen as belonging. I am Swedish, yet my name and appearance are enough to set me apart from the many cultural commonalities in Sweden.

I have realised that achieving an unambiguous understanding across cultures requires the correct method of communication. I believe that craft can speak. The practical skill of a maker can be read or heard by others without the need for words. Through material and technique, the visual communication of thoughts or the evocation of specific emotions can be created through the crafted object itself. However, I have found that it is often only by the simple guidance of words that a level of mutual understanding can be cemented when perceiving a body of work: when exposed to others' form of self-expression—to other ways of being.

The written word offers certainty.

Words are simple in that, once written, they become permanent and endure, making sure the intent behind a body of work remains clear. In my research on the basket, as narrator of its history within this publication, I want to present many and distinct perspectives on its existence, broadening the scope of its known history. I want to articulate the many facets I see as part of its being. Needless to say, (for me) one of its most notable features is its connection to my family. The basket holds our lineage: Lennart's reality and, now, my own hopes for the future.

For me, as a maker, identifying and articulating the specificities of my own culture through words (alongside weaving) has, in this publication, become the means by which I can express the core facets of my lived reality, the root cause of the said frustration: to not be perceived by one's peers as the rightful owner of our shared culture.

In the role of narrator, when using the certainty of words on behalf of the basket, my lived experience has been given space to be articulated as part of these newly written accounts. By setting the tone of my own language, I aim to convey the cultural conditions that have shaped my way of relating to making. In this section, I have gathered my most immediate thoughts on the broader divisions between my cultural context and the social environment belonging to Lennart. By articulating these specificities in print, I hope to solidify my view of the world and for it to be extended to others, whether they share my background or are part of the basket's immediate surroundings.

I quickly learned that trying to clearly communicate these elements is a process that could continue indefinitely, since all these living variables are in constant flux. I have therefore chosen to describe these words-in-print as notes. When compiled, I want these notes to be experienced as a continuous train of thought—written snapshots taken from an infinity of lived experiences that continue to fuel my *felt* need to explore the basket.

As such, these are my *personal notes on belonging*.

***

Most of the reference material found throughout this publication has been gathered from Swedish sources and translated into English by yours truly (unless an English equivalent already existed). My aim has been to convey thoughts and ideas, embrace imperfection, and carry meaning and nuance across languages.

As William H. Carpenter, translator of the book *The Slöjd in the Service of the School* (1888) by Swedish craft educator Otto Salomon, stated:

> **The English translation, it is perhaps hardly necessary to state, has been made to follow as closely as possible the letter of the original. If deviations occur they are such as were judged necessary in the change of idiom, but are, it is hoped, only in form and not in sense.[1]**

***

My mother hails from the same region as her grandfather Lennart, the Seven Districts. She was brought up in the countryside, just a stone's throw away from Risa, where 'the last basket maker' lived and worked, in the village this whole story is centred around—Hedared.

A brief geography lesson: Hedared is located in the district of Veden, one of the Seven Districts. Borås is the capital city of the districts, which in turn, lie within the greater region of Västergötland (direct translation: West Götland).

In this part of Sweden, *Götamål*,[2] a collection of regional dialects unique to the region of Västergötland (and its neighbouring areas), holds a significant presence. When spoken, *Västgötska* (Westgötska), makes itself known with immediate effect. The dialect is deeply rooted in my family. Whilst it can range in intensity, depending on where the speaker is from, its unique melody and distinct sounds are not easily ignored. People from older generations with a rural background tend to speak with a stronger dialect, as in the case of my maternal grandparents.

I come from the same region as my mother and her parents. I also speak in the same dialect. However, due to my age and the fact that I grew up in Borås, I'd argue I speak a milder form of Västgötska. My Swedish grandparents were born in the 1930s and brought up in the countryside. They fit the archetype of someone who speaks in a heavier, rural and more 'authentic' version of Västgötska. Even though the distinct locality of my dialect can be detected when I speak Swedish, I describe it as mild because, in contrast to my grandparents, my way of speaking is most definitely that: mild.

Growing up and hearing them speak, I felt at ease in Västgötska's presence, appreciating its rhythmic and harmonious melody. The dialect and its melodic tones are intrinsically linked to them—Ruth and Stig—attached to the loving sounds of their voices. Due to them both having rural origins and having lived there, in my mind, the dialect is also intertwined with the physical space of Hedared. Hearing a heavy Västgötska spoken, transports me to treasured childhood locations in the village, particularly to my grandfather's house on the street *Källstigen*. My mother's childhood home is located on the same street, just a few doors down. Stig's beige/brown house on Källstigen was the place we went to for most family gatherings, whether they were birthdays or public holidays. The melody of Västgötska filled the rooms of his house, and in these moments naturally became connected to a sense of togetherness. Its distinct sounds were also, particularly through my grandfather, made more humorous. The dialectal uniqueness found in Västgötska has often become a cause for amusement. Even my mother, who was brought up in Hedared, finds the use of certain sayings or words completely ridiculous. Its funniness made it all the more homely, and dear. I would argue that any Swedish speaker would be able to detect the inherent 'ruralness' in the ebbs and flows of Västgötska, yet still be able to decipher if the speaker was from the local capital Borås or its surrounding countryside. Since I grew up in the city, I would shy away from my natural inclination to adhere to its rhythm due to its instantaneous connection to the countryside (which as a teenager was not seen as an attractive feature).

With age, I have come to enjoy catching myself subconsciously allowing the melody of Västgötska seep into my own way of speaking. I have come to appreciate what I see as the most distinctive features of the dialect: its elongated vowels, and the not rolling but ever-enunciated r's. I now regard its sounds as an intrinsic part of who I am and my Swedish identity.

***

The typical features of Götamål are common across its geographical area, although some variations are only spoken in specific locations. In the local realm of Hedared (and its surrounding area), these not rolling but ever-enunciated r's are found. It's defined as the *Götaskorrning*. There isn't a direct English translation, instead, it could most easily be described as a regional phonetic feature, unique for Götamål—where, in this instance, the 'r' is pronounced with 'the back of the tongue'.[3] For example, the word *korg* (basket) is roughly pronounced as *kôrj*. The name of the village itself, Hedared, which in standard Swedish would generally have every letter enunciated, loses some of its consonants and is instead spoken along the lines of *Heare*.[4]

In both instances, there is an emphasis on, not rolling per se, but *enunciating* the 'r'.

korg **(basket):** [kɔrj] roughly becomes
kôrj: [kɐrj]

Hedared: [ˈheːdaˌreːd] roughly becomes
Heare: [ˈheːaˌʁeː]

In Hedared, another common feature of Västgötska is vowel transitions: for example, where the vowel 'ö' is used instead of 'y'.[5] When discussing this with my mother, we came up with an example where both dialectal features could be demonstrated, found in the pronunciation of the famed Hedared stave church. The local dialect would make the word,

kyrka **(church):** [ɕyrkɑ] become something along the lines of *körka:* [ɕørka]

Hedareds stavkyrka **(Hedared stave church):**
[ˈheːdaˌreːds ˈstɑːvˌɕyrka]
would then be spoken along the lines of
Heares stavkörka: [ˈheːaˌʁeːs ˈstɑːvˌɕørka]

It is a nearly impossible task to fully (and accurately) convey all the nuances of the dialect through text in Swedish, let alone translate it into English. Nonetheless, the above gives a brief example of how the local variation of Västgötska in Hedared deviates from standard Swedish.

Essentially, Västgötska is very distinct.

Sounding like a *Västskötte*—using local expressions such as pronouncing korg (basket) as kôrj—demonstrates an obvious belonging to Västergötland. As an observer of its heavier form and a participant in its milder iteration, I would liken the ability to speak Västgötska to being indicative of the ability to effortlessly navigate both known and unspoken cultural cues.

The dialect allows its speakers to partake in a socially and generationally established understanding that connects them to the histories and lived experiences of those who came before. It implies a shared point of view between its users, and when spoken in its heavy, melodic and *authentic* form, Västgötska often signals a political consensus, typically rooted in the speaker's rural background.

This sense of belonging, conveyed through one's speech, was naturally passed down to me by my mother and her extended family. Despite growing up in the city, I was immersed in the Eurocentric and rural norms that define Västgötska through my Swedish family—particularly when experiencing its sense of togetherness in Hedared.

***

I grew up in the borough of Hulta in Borås. The area stands divided and built on a slope. The look of the place (as we know it today) was developed in the 1960s, and its completion marked a drastic change to the surrounding landscape.[6]

A series of eight-story high-rises emerge as you drive onto the foot of Hulta's slope from the nearby motorway. Alongside these high-rises, a chain of smaller three-story buildings appears. Uniform in appearance, their distinct rectangular form stands in neat, repetitive rows across Hulta. Once at the top of the slope, a view of the traffic running along the motorway is framed next to the series of high-rises and the repetitive rows of three-story buildings.

Here, a string of privately-owned properties runs along the left side of the slope, until you, again, meet the high-rises and the accompanying three-story buildings (and the sound of the traffic) at its foot. Prior to its housing developments,

Hulta was regarded as pure countryside, with farms and market gardens, which is still a noticeable fact with the nearby green areas and its closeness to the forest. Growing up in the early noughties, I would describe Hulta as defined by these high-rises—dense, concrete-poured structures that almost feel monumental. These buildings are often characterised by their balconies, neatly arranged in vertical lines across their facade, and frequently adorned with as many parabolic antennas as actual residents.

Together, these buildings stand as remnants of the so-called *Miljonprogrammet* ('The Million Programme'), an ambitious public housing scheme implemented in Sweden between the mid-1960s to the mid-1970s.[7]

The expression miljonprogrammet was not in regard to an actual programme for increased housing production [...] rather it was more about highlighting that there was a stated [political] goal to further increase the rate of housing production, and how it was done— by building more rationally and industrially.

The housing shortage was an important political issue throughout the post-war period. The economic boom after World War II [with population growth and urbanisation] increased the demand for housing. [...] Housing construction during miljonprogrammet was heavily regulated. Since almost all construction was realised with the help of state subsidies, production was steered through the grants approved by Parliament.[8]

Lamell-buildings, housing with three floors, were by far the most common house type. The [general] criticism against high-rises was based on the high rate of exploitation and on the fact that there was 'a large concentration of people on a small area of land'. At the same time, a high density of housing was necessary to accommodate the residents' demands for service.[9]

Many of those who moved into a newly built home were happy to finally have a home after many years on the housing waiting list, to stop living in overcrowded conditions, and to enjoy a better standard of housing than they had before. However, [the critics remained many]: rents were too high, services and communications were inadequate, and the areas were too unilaterally designed, with their outdoor environments forgotten. The cost of building quickly and cheaply resulted in recurring social and physical interventions, which have not been able to improve the areas' lack of attractiveness on the housing market.[10]

The flats of miljonprogrammet are often well-planned and functional. Today, many are in great need of upgrade to not reach the end of their lifespan, with the renewal of windows, balconies, and facades.[11]

Lamell-buildings, housing with three floors... I know these far too well, as I grew up in such a building. I have first-hand experience with the 'functionality' of this kind of miljonprogrammet flat. On the street where I grew up, there are multiple lamell-buildings, and their uniform exterior is hard to miss. Stretching across the right side of Hulta's slope, making up *Skillingsgatan* (Skilling Street), these lamell-buildings separate themselves from other three-story structures in the area, mostly in appearance, but more by the fact that these are not solely rental properties but include privately-owned flats. Regardless of ownership type, instead of their rectangular form being placed in repetitive rows, they are arranged in bracket-like formations, with five identical structures repeated five times across the side of the slope.

I vividly remember when the rental lamell-properties on Skillingsgatan received their facelift. These renovations replaced the previously exposed yellow brick and green woodish plates (that covered their exterior) with black wooden panels with contrasting sections in white. This accentuated the buildings' distinct and somewhat harsh, semi-brutalist features. The exterior on the 'inside' of the buildings' bracket-like shape was covered in white wooden panels with sections in complementary yellow.

Their internal layout follows a similar uniform pattern to the building's exterior. If you were to go inside one of the flats, opening its front door and looking down as you entered, you would be met with floors continuously covered in variations of linoleum carpet, with the exception of the oak herringbone parquet in the living room.

The walls inside the flat would be wallpapered, not painted, covered in a selection of options provided by the landlord/housing company. A two-bedroom flat has a rectangular entrance hallway. At the end of the hallway, a doorway to the left leads into a similarly rectangular kitchen, which opens into a more square-shaped living room with an adjoining rectangular balcony. If instead turning right at the end of the hallway, you'd find a small, square landing with three doors: one for each bedroom and the third leading to a bathroom.

Out on the balcony, you'd stand on poured concrete, surrounded by poured concrete. The continuous poured concrete abruptly transitions to a section of exposed black metal fencing. This section of the balcony gives an undisrupted view of the outside plot of green grass centred in the middle of the building, enclosed by the bracket-shaped structure itself.

***

In the series of books *Historien om Borås stadsbebyggelse* (roughly translated: 'The history of Borås' urban development'), the second instalment opens with a section of its preface reading:

> **In a city like Borås, our forefathers' ideas and visions, as well as their economic and social conditions, have left their mark in the form of streets and houses. With the houses and streets as a starting point, much can therefore be told and explained about the city and the people who once lived here.[12]**

The opening chapter *Med trångboddhet som drivkraft* ('With overcrowding as a driving force') describes how the years around 1930 appear to mark a turning point for Sweden regarding the perception of the home and housing in general.[13] At the time, Sweden was a country riddled with overcrowded, meagre, and insubstantial housing. There was a widespread desire to develop Sweden from *Fattigsverige* (the old and impoverished) into a modern and prosperous democracy.

The willingness for change in society was strong and shared by both right- and left-wing politicians, as well as by industry, among its shareholders and labourers.[14]

Author Fredrik Hjelm quotes a 1938 publication by *Hyresgästernas Riksförbund* and *Borås Hyresgästförening* (roughly translated: the National Association of Tenants with the local Borås Association) stating:

> **Overcrowding in our country is a social disease of immense proportions. It means increased risks of disease, but above all an increased danger to mental well-being.[15]**

Quoted in the same publication is 'psychological expert' Alva Myrdal who furthered such notions:

Overall, the unavoidable togetherness in both big and small matters, in conflicts, arguments and eroticism, in hymn-singing and card games, rest and vigil, becomes nerve-wracking for everyone. The comfort in living together becomes difficult to achieve. Irritation becomes inevitable when solitude can never be offered as an alternative to togetherness. If any family member suffers from nervousness, alcoholism, or temperamental peculiarities, there is no way to retreat. Everything must be shared by all, everything must be experienced by all. Moral contagion is made easier. A cramped home lowers the individual's well-being and ability to work, ultimately undermining a healthy and harmonious home life—this is, in the end, the human reality behind the statistics.[16]

Simply put, the home was becoming a vital part of a functioning family unit: a central component in the making of the Swedish welfare state. Hjelm continues:

...Miljonprogrammet significantly boosted housing construction. Never before had so many homes been built in Sweden as during the 1960s, which led to an improvement in housing standards. [...] The norm for what was considered overcrowded was changed in 1965, to define households where more than two people per room lived, excluding not only the kitchen but the living room as well.[17]

***

Most observers probably thought that the welfare state of Sweden would not have to experience widespread overcrowding again. However, with more families, due to high housing prices, either being made or choosing to stay in smaller apartments in city centres, coupled with new, larger family formations, primarily among immigrant groups with low incomes, the issue of overcrowding has once again become relevant. The extent of it, however, is not comparable to what Sweden previously experienced. Since 1982, the norm for what is considered overcrowded has been defined as where more than one person is living per room—kitchen and living room excluded! Today, Swedes are, overall, among the people in the world with the most living space per person.[18]

Hulta exists like a microcosm, built of a seemingly infinite amount of cultural expressions. It is where migrated cultures coexist. I often think that Hulta's artificial environment hinders its cultural richness to flourish and its lessons of coexistence to transcend to the general culture of Västgötska—for a genuine experience to occur between the two. For within its miljonprogram, held within its high-rises, lies a whole world in itself. Its many cultures exist so condensed across its slope that its various expressions: customs, traditions and languages, like planetary bodies, continuously clash, ignite, and merge to fuel its own energy—one that can only be described as in constant motion: elusive and multiple.

As a miljonprogrammet native, the actuality of social hierarchies is an experience I carry with me. I have met its sense of limitation within the borders of Hulta, between the many cultures occupying its slope, but even more so when facing the outside world and its status quo (Västgötska).

It has taught me that however many lessons of coexistence or insightful abilities are fostered by growing up in miljonprogrammet, the faceless plurality of its artificial environment repeatedly fails to be applied, recognised, or adopted by the greater culture of Sjuhärad.

Hulta's energy, confined but in endless motion, continuously birthing new expressions, feeds its lived experience as one defined by a search—forwards, upwards, away from itself—an endless pursuit towards a final form in which to exist. Amongst this sea of expressions, all wanting to enable themselves to transcend the confines of their concrete-steeped environment, understanding one's relationality to the outside world becomes of the utmost importance.

The internalised process of gauging across cultural barriers becomes normalised, and the reality of social hierarchies accepted as fact, when the pursuit of transcendence is only made possible by acts of self-erasure.

In my experience, transcendence—to become regarded as equal—is a rare gift. While it means the end of searching, to no longer be defined by an endless pursuit but to be rooted and anchored, it comes at a price. Transcendence knows how to translate the inherent motion of one's roots, the seemingly infinite amounts of cultural expressions of one's core being, into the still and singular of the status quo (Västgötska).

The insightful ability to understand one's relationality to the outside world stays limited to the borders of miljonprogrammet. It remains confined until the opportunity presents itself, to showcase one's ability, applying adequate amounts of self-erasure to be recognised as familiar, and embraced by those already embodying what being true *truly* means (Västgötska).

***

Hulta is classified as a *särskilt utsatt område* ('particularly vulnerable area') by the Swedish authorities.[19] Divided into three sections, the classification ranges from:

utsatt område —'vulnerable area'

riskområde —'at risk area'

to the highest:

30

särskilt utsatt område —'particularly vulnerable area'

A 'vulnerable area' is a geographically defined area characterised by its low socioeconomic status, where criminals influence the local community. This influence is tied to the social context of the area rather than an explicit intention to gain power and control over the local community. It can manifest as direct pressure, such as threats and extortion, or indirect effects, including:

* public acts of violence risking harm to the general public
* drug trafficking openly conducted
* an outward-acting dissatisfaction with society

As a result, residents experience a lack of safety, which in turn reduces their willingness to report crime and participate in legal processes. The situation is considered *serious*.[20]

An 'at risk area' meets all the criteria for a 'vulnerable area' but does not yet meet the criteria for a 'particularly vulnerable area'. However, the situation is so serious that there is an imminent risk of it becoming 'particularly vulnerable' if appropriate measures are not implemented.[21] The situation is considered *alarming*.[22]

A 'particularly vulnerable area' is characterised by a general unwillingness to participate in legal processes. Systematic threats and acts of violence against witnesses, victims, and those who report crimes may also occur. The situation makes it difficult, if not nearly impossible, for the police to carry out their duties. In many

**cases, the situation in the area has become normalised, meaning that neither the police nor residents actively reflect on its severity.
The situation is considered *critical*.[23]**

Hedared was one of the first places I experienced what cultural uniformity looked like, but more importantly, what it *felt* like. Whereas I perceived my native Hulta as in constant cultural flux, Hedared stood as its opposite: singular and static. My experience of Hulta is defined by its sense of motion, transformation, betterment—a constant reach forwards, upwards: away from itself. It is hard to pinpoint one form of culture when a place is everything, everywhere, all at once.

I perceived Hedared as a place of stillness in that, unlike Hulta, its culture was made by elements of permanence, tangibly scattered throughout the village. Found in traditions like the basket or in historical buildings standing intact since the Dark Ages. Its strong sense of lineage, found in artefacts and its built environment, continues to inform the many commonalities among its inhabitants. By spending time in Hedared throughout my upbringing, I learnt that living close to one's roots means not having to chase them but being able to perceive, comprehend and effortlessly become one with them. They are as much part of the past as they are of the present. In a place like Hedared, one's roots are not only for you to perceive, understand, and experience: they are apparent and comprehensible to the world around you. You stem from said place. You speak in your ancestors' tongue, bear their name, stand on their ground, and look out over their land.

Experiencing the foundational sources of one's roots not only renders family histories real, but offers a stable foundation for building an identity. This grounding effect, shaped by tangible connections, influences how one navigates the world. The tangible sensing of home calms the internal search for place, belonging, and truth—especially when that sense is affirmed by the outside world.

Across generations, Hedared's identity is formed by the continuous experience of the familiar, a shared cultural consensus interwoven throughout the community. In my mind, in contrast to Hulta, Hedared serves as the archetype of a place where the born-and-bred cultural context of Västgötska exists. For me, the village was where it originated and continues to reside, practised and articulated by *true* natives.

Hence why, as an outsider looking in, I perceived the village as a place of the permanent. A place to know, believe and adhere to tradition—a place of *true* roots, with Västgötska as its native language.

***

The monotonous, concrete-poured walls of Hulta have little in common with other parts of Sjuhärad. The policy-driven forces of 'rationality and function' that planned miljonprogrammet gave way for its uniform developments to stand within their own cultural blank space. Its monumental high-rises (and the emerging cultures connected to them) are still relatively young.

The man-made elements of miljonprogrammet continue to bring a sense of tension to Sjuhärad. Its immediate otherness is, at first glance, reflected in the distinct look of the place: its faceless environments evoke a sense of the unfamiliar. The residents inhabiting these environments second what is perceived as hard to understand and disconnected from the cultural norms of Västgötska.

Yet, despite the inherent sense of cultural ambiguity and the defaulted facelessness of Hulta's environment, amongst the monotonous and densely populated high-rises, the roots of the local region remain intact.

The names given to the streets occupied by these monumental structures draw a direct parallel between the artifice of today and the rich craft histories of the past.

***

Knallar were historical merchants from the Sjuhärad region in Västergötland. They travelled across Sweden (and the Nordics) to sell the handcrafted goods made in the Seven Districts.

Knallarna travelled largely by foot (when trading smaller goods) and often used horse and carriage when having larger inventories to sell, and would, in that case, bring along a so-called *handelsdräng* (trades apprentice) to accompany them. On their voyages from region to region, a need to protect business interests arose when speaking with apprentices or other peers, and knallarna developed their own way of speaking, their own 'secret language', *Månsing*.[24] It was never a complete language. Instead, it originally consisted of several dialectal words taken from Västgötska (often already hard to understand for outsiders), then distorted and made interchangeable.[25] With time, it came to incorporate parts taken from neighbouring languages of nearby countries, which were mixed into the otherwise 'correct speech' to make it incomprehensible to outsiders.[26]

In the book *Månsing: knallarna's secret language* (2004), author Sven H. G. Lagerström breaks down Månsing's origins, usage, and eventual decline:

> The phenomenon is by no means unique to knallarna. The chimney sweeps had their [own jargon], and the leather workers in Malung [in north Sweden] and the surrounding areas developed what is known as Skinnamål. [...] With time, [Månsing] came to include words from several languages. Another element was the frequent use of various metaphors and semantic shifts. Out on the roads, knallarna naturally came into contact with many lawless vagrants, which made for the number of words in Månsing to increase. The Romani people, who have been travelling in Sweden since the 1500s, were another group they encountered, and several words from their language, Romani, enriched Månsing as well. All of this, of course, means that Månsing, like Swedish and other languages, developed gradually over the centuries it was spoken. Therefore, it is not accurate to

speak of 'authentic' Månsing as opposed to the Månsing spoken during knallarna's final active years.[27]

Although not immediately apparent, the names of the streets going across Hulta's slope directly reference Månsing and connect the area to the ways of speaking in the historical cottage industry. Lagerström includes a dictionary of Månsing,[28] and when driving off the nearby motorway, onto the foot of Hulta's slope, onto *Hultagatan* (Hulta Street), you come across (in no particular order):

Blejdegatan (Blejde Street)
Blejd(e) — A twenty-five-*öre* (pence) coin. A blejd(e) was a wedge, like the piece one cuts out when felling a tree. The twenty-five-öre coin was perceived as something carved out of the higher denomination, the Swedish krona.

Fessingsgatan (Fessing Street)
Fässing — *Fässingen/fessingen/fös(s)ingen* was the sack that the knalle carried over their shoulder.

Hansinggatan (Hansing Street)
Hansing — Silver, from the term for a small silver coin.

Månsinggatan (Månsing Street)
Månsing — The language of knallarna.

Skillingsgatan (Skilling Street) [29]
Skilling — Currency unit in Sweden from 1777 to 1855.

In 1864, favourable tax benefits for Borås-based merchants were abolished, leading to a sharp decline in travelling knallar. The practice had more or less entirely died out during

the first decades of the twentieth century. The trade itself,
however, persisted and took on new forms.[30]

Lagerström continues:

> Naturally, not all knallar were familiar with
> every word, on the contrary, some words were
> likely used only in limited circles. While certain
> Månsing words appear in multiple records,
> some have only been documented in a handful
> of cases. Nils Hufwedsson Dal includes a short
> glossary of the most common words in his
> [book] *Boërosia* (1719). In *Dialectus Vestrogothi-
> ca* (1772), Sven Hof lists a number of words that
> have been 'revealed'.[31]

***

> A year after the abolition of the special trade
> regulations in 1864 [priest and prominent figure
> in historic Västgötsk literature], Claës Johan
> Ljungström wrote about Månsing: 'With each
> passing year, it dies out more and more, and as
> it is both a linguistic and moral monstrosity,
> its demise is a loss to no one.'[32]

FÖRORTSSVENSKA

In Sweden, before having an in-person interaction, my roots
from elsewhere are evident by simply deciphering my name
through text. Mourali doesn't resemble Pettersson in the
slightest. I was first made aware of this during my first week
of school. I was put in a group, separate from the main class,
alongside other students with 'Mourali-clinging' surnames
(fellow students who also lived within miljonprogrammet).
We had all been placed in an extra class for students with
Swedish as a second language. I remember thinking nothing of
it, but at the same time, feeling a bit confused. Why am I being

taught the basics of my own language? My grandparents spoke in rural, *authentic* Västgötska, and I didn't even speak a second language beyond my milder iteration. The only criterion for me being included in this group was my name, Fadhel.

My mother was furious. Through such (seemingly minuscule) cultural mix-ups with other owners of Västgötska, her children were made different from herself. In her eyes, Mourali was naturally equal to Pettersson. Continuing to experience and observe this web of perception play out between my two cultures, time and time again (each time under new circumstances) made my ability to gauge my surroundings. It fuelled my continuous search—away from myself, to affirm and prove my belonging—beyond a place where one's family lives on linoleum-covered floors (or has a parabolic antenna attached to their concrete-poured balcony).

I learnt that it was more important for me to prove my perfect dialect (and cultural adherence to Västgötska) than it was for my peers with names like Lennart to be able to pronounce mine. I often felt I was in debt, needing to reassure people with an unsure tone of my belonging that despite my name, I was part of the common ground of Västgötska.

My Swedish identity is defined by my inability to speak Arabic, a fact that is constantly present in my name, Fadhel. While it distances me from the joint camaraderie of my primary culture, my *felt* belonging to Tunisia is affirmed, again and again, through my name.

Fadhel Hamdi ben Azzedine Mourali.

***

My father is the second eldest in a family of eight siblings. He was born in 1956 in the countryside in Tunisia, the same year the country became independent from its French colonisers. Sweden became his permanent place of residence in the late 1970s, not out of urgent refuge but as the place he found love. And as they say, the rest is history.

One of the reasons for my trepidation about the (perceived to be) conditioned camaraderie of Västgötska comes from understanding my father's cultural manoeuvring from being an immigrant in Sweden.

I return to a story told by my parents when they first became an item. On one of my father's first visits to Hedared, the attitude towards his very apparent non-Västgötska appearance ended in violence. Before the escalation, he was denied entry to a function in the village and called slurs, not by people who were part of my immediate family, but by people within the circle of trust that is Västgötska. Having this story retold in detail, seeing how my parents dealt with the outside world and its perceptions of their relationship has, naturally, also informed my view of the world.

When my father left Tunisia, he did so for Italy in his late teens and sought employment in hospitality. He then worked in hospitality his whole life as a restaurateur. I grew up in the back-of-house of countless establishments, familiar with the delivery docks at the back, the kilo sacks of produce, the storage spaces, the big industrial dishwasher and the sous-chef going through a pack-a-day (not to forget the endless boredom of people-watching). My father was a chef by trade. He was also the restaurant owner, head of operations, and face of the front-of-house. He did everything. My siblings and I spent hours on end in the various establishments he ran at different points in time during our childhood. My father is very good with people. His sense of humour is a key personality trait. Whether interacting with regulars at the restaurant, the local grocer, or the owner of the neighbouring café, he would always charm the people around him. I observed and saw how laughter could be disarming. Dad had mastered the art of navigating his otherness, and found his relationship with Västgötska, through humour—skillfully manoeuvring around prejudice and its potential consequences.

***

In the three-story lamell-building I grew up, there were six flats in each of the eleven stairwells. Each flat (depending on size) was laid out in a similar design as previously described, with its walls covered in standardised wallpapers and its floors clad in linoleum carpet (except for the living room with its oak herringbone parquet). On our front door, my mother's surname, Pettersson, stood out as one of few doors bearing such a name—one that was *not* 'Mourali-clinging' (foreign-sounding to the average Västskötte). In general, based on appearance, there was a distinct lack of what would be considered traditionally Västgötskt within my immediate family, and amongst our neighbours too. The families next door looked, spoke, dressed, and were certainly named differently from me and my family. They simply existed in a different way than us, right next door. Early on, I understood that multiple ways to see and be in the world existed. If anything, this was a fact in our own home, having the Swedish and Tunisian cultures coexisting within our four walls.

Within the cultural coexistence of Hulta, the rurality and uniformity of Västgötska often felt distant, yet it was the only language spoken in our home. My father tongue, Arabic, existed, but only in the periphery. Beyond the general greeting, my closest connection to it was still my name. Although present in its milder iteration, what took preface over the melodic sounds of Västgötska in Hulta—a cultural melting pot in constant flux, shaped by the man-made nature of miljon-programmet, classified as a particularly vulnerable area—was *Förortssvenska*. The word *förort* translates to 'suburb' in English. The word *Svenska* means 'Swedish'. It would directly translate into 'Suburban Swedish', but rather than referencing a picturesque suburb with white picket fences, the term förort typically refers to places like Hulta, to miljonprogrammet. When leaving our flat, its sounds would surround me.

Förortssvenska transforms the concrete-steeped visuals of Hulta into audio. In my late teens, I had developed a more objective understanding of my father's cultural manoeuvring. As an adult, I can now see why my only language growing up was a mild Västgötska. My father wanted me, as the next generation, to adhere to a primary culture, to have the opportunity to transcend, to fit in and to belong—a privilege he was not afforded.

Swedish typically follows the V2 (verb-second) word order,[33] meaning that the verb appears in the second position in a sentence. For example, in English:

'today, she makes a basket'

 becomes

'idag gör hon en korg' in Swedish.

If you were to directly translate it back into English, it would read as:

'today, makes she a basket'

The verb gör (makes) appears in the second position, demonstrating the V2 (verb-second) word order in standard Swedish. Förortssvenska is not a uniform language variant, but can vary significantly between different areas, groups and speakers. However, there are some common linguistic features.[34] In the rhythm of Förortssvenska, the V2 rule is often relaxed, where the subject might come before the verb .

The phrase 'today, she makes a basket'

would in Förortssvenska, directly mirror the English way of speaking, and be spoken along the lines of:

'idag hon gör en korg'

which would follow the typical pattern of the V3 (verb-third) word order. Swedish then has a similar structure to English.[35]

For someone learning Swedish, using the V2 rule can be particularly challenging to adopt. In terms of understanding, it matters little. There are many examples where the V2 rule is disregarded in native speakers' Swedish, so [Swedes] are hardly unfamiliar with hearing V3 sentences. [...] The type of V3 sentences used by native speakers are not perceived as symbolically problematic, but V3 sentences that are not part of those used by native speakers do carry a strong symbolic value. [...] Its symbolism is determined by who places the verb in the third position, and the attitude of the listener.[36]

Essentially, Förortssvenska, too, much like Västgötska, is very distinct.

Sometimes Förortssvenska is mistakenly perceived as a foreign accent. This would imply that the speakers have Swedish as a second language and that their Swedish pronunciation is influenced by their mother tongue. Förortssvenska is not an accent, it is a variant of Swedish spoken by both monolingual and multilingual individuals.[37]

A historical parallel to today's Förortssvenska is the so-called *Ekensnacket*, or *Söderslangen*, which was spoken among the working class in Stockholm[38] (which also has ties to Månsing).[39] Today, many think of Ekensnacket as a kind of authentic Stockholm dialect, but in actuality, it is a sociolect that emerged among young people in working-class areas on the outskirts of Stockholm, which developed alongside the large influx of people [into the city] around the turn of the twentieth century.[40]

Förortssvenska is not just characterised by how its sentences are built, it is defined by its vocabulary. There are a plethora of words used in Förortssvenska that are borrowed from other languages.

My use of this vocabulary is limited. I grew up in the small town of Borås, had I been brought up in a miljonprogram outside of big cities like Stockholm or Gothenburg, it probably would have had a heavier influence on my way of speaking. Since I grew up in the mid-noughties, I would argue that the widespread use of its vocabulary has since become more common, most notably through popular culture.

Below is a list of Förortssvenska words. It's important to note that this is not an exhaustive list—it includes words compiled by me, with the help of family and friends of a similar age, after reflecting together on the language we were exposed to while growing up in Borås about twenty years ago:

Aboow — 'wow' or 'oh my god'
Aboow, this basket is coiled!

Aina — 'the cops', 'the police'
Ey, aina is coming, hide the pine!

Çok — Turkish word meaning 'a lot' or 'very'
En çok stor korg would roughly translate to *a very big basket.*

Fett — directly translates to 'fat' or 'grease' (used to emphasise a large quantity of something)
Fett med fur would roughly translate to *a lot of pine.*

Hayawān — Arabic word meaning 'animal' (used as an insult, but has a humorous tone to it)
Stop being such a hayawān, and continue coiling!

Hajde — derived from the Balkan languages, commonly used to mean 'let's go', 'come on' or 'hurry up'
Hajde, let's start coiling!

Suedi — simply a Swedish person (i.e. someone of Västgötsk descent)
It's only Suedis making förnings baskets.

Jalla — Arabic word (Swedish spelling) commonly used to mean 'let's go', 'come on' or 'hurry up'
Jalla, finish coiling!

Yani — an equivalent to 'like' or 'kind of'
The pine used in the Hedared basket, yani, it's hard to get.

I liken the rhythm of Förortssvenska to the height of the high-rises found in Hulta. Its melody is vast yet repetitive and structured. For me, its many sounds transport me back to the middle of Hulta's slope in the height of summer, surrounded by a group of friends and the setting sun—looking out at the monumental high-rises, their balconies and the endless parabolic antennas.

In such a moment, the sounds of Förortssvenska connect to the continuous cracking of 'bezr' shells (roasted sunflower seeds—if you know, you know) and its melody carry the flavour of the shell's salty outer coating.

Förortssvenska embodies the energy of Hulta. It is as hard and textured as the poured concrete yet as soft and smooth as the linoleum-coated floors. Its sounds tell the story of its untraceable roots. It is infused with experience, with the ability to approach and regard the world through multiple cultural filters. It echoes the universal experience of knowing others as your own by knowing yourself as other—the immense (internal) experience of not being perceived to belong.

During my upbringing, I would observe and take note of how my family members (those not named Mourali) perceived someone who looked like me—a person born in Sweden to a parent(s) who had migrated or who were immigrants themselves—other people with hard-to-pronounce names like Fadhel. It's a kind of out-of-body experience to see loved ones embrace you while dismissing other 'Fadhels' simply because we are family, by the fact that I can correctly use vowel transitions and roll my r's accordingly.

Listening to my Västgötska family members talk about their perceptions of others' ways of being often made their prejudiced nature very clear. For me, it came across as an unwillingness to accept their own unfamiliarity with things that, for them, were other. When having to pronounce new names or understand the customs of different cultures, their inherent discomfort and steadfast reluctance to embrace anything that didn't fit into their narrow perception of what Västgötska should be, made itself known time and time again. Their adverse reaction to all things 'other' further shaped my view of Västgötska as having rigid social expectations. It fed my perception of Västgötska as a very conditional way of being, while it also informed my ability to manoeuvre within its camaraderie—which seemingly wanted to be extremely homogeneous.

I was born into Västgötska, but whenever my Swedish family members pronounced my or my siblings' names, the dialect's natural flow and melodic rhythm had to shift.

My name's distinct sound gave me only limited access to the sense of community found in Västgötska. Through my name, the duality of my identity became inescapable. My name alone, even within my family, continued to set me apart as someone with roots from elsewhere. I associated my name with their discomfort with otherness. Even though I am a native Swede, my name, Fadhel, not only made me feel like an outsider but certainly made *me* feel discomfort as it disrupted *their* natural rhythm when speaking.

My name then felt like a thorn in the eye of the cultural consensus within Västgötska—and, by extension, my Swedish family. Yet, I was undeniably a part of it.

Lagom is a Swedish word that doesn't have an English translation. It describes something that is *just right*—neither too much nor too little, without exaggeration.[41] The term can apply to both things and actions, indicating that something is exactly as it should be, at just the right time or with just the right amount.

It can also be applied to behaviours: to be in *just* such a way, neither too much nor too little, just right, *without* exaggeration; embodying a way of being that is moderate, balanced, and appropriate to a given situation.[42]

In essence, lagom reflects a general approach to life that values sufficiency, calm, and proportion—what is proper, fitting, and suitable for a particular purpose.

THOUGHTS ON FAITH

Beyond stemming from different language trees, I've always found that what differentiates the two languages closest to me, Swedish and Arabic, is the articulated presence of faith.

Sweden is a secular country and Swedish is a secular language. In Sweden, I would describe faith as a quiet constant, something that is silently embedded into the fabric of society. In Swedish culture, faith makes its presence known to mark the occasion of a monumental moment in life and only reveals itself within its allocated spaces. Faith does not reside within one's home, nor is it rooted in everyday language.

A place of worship serves as a backdrop for the customary acts of life to play out: a christening, wedding, or funeral. Here, the presence of, and engagement with faith only occur in the company of others. Places of worship are collectively occupied, in moments of immense emotion—in utter despair or sheer joy—in *collective* celebration or *collective* mourning.

45

In Sweden, faith, and the places where it resides, are mere tools with a tangible function. Once the moment monumental passes and the customary act is completed, the collective leaves its allocated space and secular life resumes, until the next time faith has a functional duty to fulfil.

In Arabic, faith is not only articulated but spoken with intent and interwoven into its very structure. Its articulation is given even more room through body language: in greetings, well-wishes, expressions of hope, gratitude, or condemnation. The presence of faith in Arabic does not translate into Swedish, nor does it translate to the cultural framework of lagom.

Performing the cultural act of lagom, through both language and behaviour, involves a constant gauging of its borders, of being *just right*. I find this to be particularly true after having observed my cultures continuously interact during my upbringing. I now realise that the often subconscious act of observing became an internalised experience, where I approached Arabic from a place of longing. I wanted to be able to decipher its many sounds, which to me was as foreign as it was familiar.

The articulated presence of faith enabled me to feel connected to the many aspects of Tunisian culture that often felt out of reach, due to my inability to speak my father tongue.

Inshallah — 'God willing'

Alhamdulillah — 'praise be to God'

Bismillah — 'in the name of God'

These words surrounded me throughout my childhood, and still today, as someone who was brought up in a very secular household, in a very secular country, connects me to the normalities of Tunisian culture.

***

I find it hard to give an example. Still, when reflecting on faith, the first thing that came to mind was when my Tunisian grandfather completed his *Hajj* (the pilgrimage to Mecca, a monumental moment for any devoted Muslim). Afterwards, he was referred to as 'Hajj'—a title given as a symbol of respect, in recognition of his pilgrimage.

I was in my early teens, and I vividly remember a close Swedish family member overhearing me and my mother speaking about his second pilgrimage to Mecca when they asked: *why would you call him 'Hajj'?*

I was surprised by the question. Surely, everyone knows why?

— *Is that the equivalent to sir?*

***

I remember this as one of the first times when what is undeniably Tunisian came in clear contrast with what is undeniably Swedish. The commemoration of a religious act through a title, an epithet, or a sign of respect that differentiates an individual from others, is simply unheard of in Sweden. To let faith take centre stage, out of its veiled presence, out of its allocated spaces (without a tangible function) is not an act of lagom.

Being rooted in two cultures means having the ability to keep two conflicting thoughts in your mind at the same time. I don't believe the question was riddled with prejudice. Why would my Swedish family members know anything adjacent to faith when secularity is second nature? Still, that brief moment was more of an awakening for me, that feeling of: *Oh, they don't get it.* The interaction made me reflect on the broader differences between Swedish and Tunisian culture; if this well-educated person doesn't know 'Hajj', they certainly would not be familiar with Eid, nor would they understand the true meaning of Ramadan.

The sought-after mutual core between my two cultures kept getting lost in translation.

Much like my name, the simple articulation of faith enables me to feel a sense of true connection to Tunisia.

Uttering its words brings me closer to my roots, yet distances me from my native language and what is supposedly my primary culture.

FINDING PLACE, ROOTED IN CRAFT

I have always been (subconsciously, I think) drawn to craft; when feeling unsure of where my true place of belonging is in the world, I think its allure is found in the way craft affirms a universal consensus to a process. Craft presents an absolute way of doing: a set of unshakeable principles made comprehensible through a tactile and regimented process.

When feeling confined to only exist within the borders of the in-betweenship, the crafting process offers a sense of certainty, something unquestionable. Its qualities mirror my own search for belonging: a safe space, a stable foundation from which to build an identity, shaped by something equally as definitive. The basket is found amidst this definite and universal way of practice. Its heritage so clearly exemplifies the inherent qualities of craft: how an absolute process can inform identity, represent lineage, and offer a sense of community all at the same time.

It is in the absolute ways of the Hedared basket that we find Lennart. He turns the basket, and by extension, the definite ways of craft, into a personal matter. As Lennart's great-grandson, I have gained access to its lineage of makers, not as a basket maker myself, but as the narrator of its story within this publication. I have been allowed to wallow in its tradition, and through its continued practice, been able to examine the universal and unshakable principles of craft in action. I have gotten to observe how its practice has unfolded, been adapted, and evolved into a source of community.

I have been given time to dissect the basket's regimented process, tease out its composition of local histories, and give a face to the hands that have made it.

The objects Lennart left behind continue to represent his reality, one that was defined by necessity, and shaped by the authoritative nature of craft. Like Lennart, I know what it feels like to have your existence be conditioned by outside elements. I grew up a queer kid named Fadhel in a small town in west Sweden, constantly trying to navigate around the culturally correct way of doing things. I can certainly see parts of myself in him. We both had to adhere to set ways of doing things simply because 'that's the way it is'.

In the Pettersson/Mourali family, the need to make in order to survive is a thing of the past. Yet, nearly half a century after his passing, my relationship with craft still stems from necessity: to find a place of belonging where my lived experience is articulated and made equal.

The in-betweenness I inherently inhabit is not a relic of the past but a reality firmly rooted in the present. Hulta is a relatively young place, one that does not have an object derived from its land, that for generations has been made into a conduit for common experiences: a vessel made with universal principles, processed through local hands. The faceless, man-made landscapes of Hulta lack tangible objects that embody its story, artefacts that, beyond words, can convey its realities to the outside world.

The culture that shaped Lennart, along with its present-day remnants, can be understood within a broader context through the universal principles of craft. His baskets, derived from his conditional mode of practice, were reasons for the world around him to write accounts, collect communal stories, and record other forms of documentation, which further cemented the greater social and cultural reality of his life.

In the process of Förortssvenska becoming its own recognised, trusted, and comprehended way of being, the established traditions (craft or otherwise) surrounding Lennart serve as the perfect measuring tool. By immersing myself in his life and practice, I can position craft as a mirror, adopting its cemented, authoritative, and absolute nature within my own cultural context. Though our histories have unfolded across different generations, craft serves as a universal and recognisable point of reference, anchoring and unifying our lineage. My desire to practice weaving stems from a need to transform my inherent in-betweenness into something as tangible and *definite* as the basket. In the absence of a universal consensus; an understanding that can extend to the outside world (in the form of a crafted object or otherwise), my native culture stays not a tangible 'thing', but a fleeting, and *felt* experience.

The culture of Förortssvenska remains the David to Västgötska's Goliath.

***

Through craft, I am connected to my heritage whilst being free to affirm my own sense of self. Yet, discovering the tools to bring this process to life has been a journey in and of itself.

It wasn't until the end of my undergraduate degree that I had acquired the perspectives on craft needed to start putting together the pieces of this puzzle. When I began to understand craft as a cultural process, the basket became a vessel for deciphering my own lived experience. It is because of the basket's personal connection that I was comfortable enough to confront the foreign nature of its traditions. Because the heritage of the basket is part of my lineage, I realised I had agency to subvert it.

Having access to craft and understanding the variables that allow me to regard it as a gateway to self-expression is a matter of privilege. Growing up among the concrete-steeped environments of Hulta, I was so far removed from all that Hedared embodied that an artisanal tradition like the basket would only seem alien to the everyday. At university, these pieces came into place only after a long process of transcending concrete.

***

When attending upper secondary school in my hometown of Borås (the city, which you will later become more familiar with, is renowned in Sweden for its former textile industry), I studied a 'textile and clothing' course. It was primarily practical. Over three years, I was taught the basics of sewing, pattern cutting, and given a general knowledge of textile fibres

50

and their procurement processes. The course was designed to provide foundational knowledge in each subject, enabling students to specialise in a chosen area after graduation.

I always thought fashion was the end destination. I have found that with many textile designers, fashion seemed to be the only option when acquiring such skills. In comparison to working with textiles, the end destination of fashion is instantaneous and familiar. We all have a perception of what clothes are. Clothing is part of everyday life. Understanding textiles, much like understanding the Hedared basket, requires prior knowledge. Finding my way to weaving has, indeed, been a long journey.

While fashion captivated me with its grandeur and promise of something other (than the confines of a small town in the countryside of west Sweden), I understood that knowing the bare bones of a garment was essential if I were to pursue such a career. Naturally, after graduation, I sought an apprenticeship in men's tailoring.

During my one-year stint in tailoring, I gained first-hand experience from a master tailor who was way past his retirement age but still going strong. He had a sharp eye and steady hand guiding his making with the highest of precision. It was a male-coded space to work in, surrounded by tradition and heritage—things not to be meddled with. All the elements that guided the tailoring process: the base pattern pieces for the suits, the wool fabrics, the scissors, the specific stitches, and the smell of the iron-steamed horse hair used to shape a jacket, were all tried and true components of its own absolute way.

Hanging on one of the walls was a red banner with the proverb:

gör rätt från början — 'do it right from the beginning'

It was a world of order where the master tailor, his apprentices, the clients, the tools, techniques, and materials all had their place. The distinction between making a good or a bad decision was very clear. We were three apprentices working in a small attic space opposite the Swedish School of Textiles in Borås. I enjoyed the rigidity of learning all its methods and techniques but felt a bit ambivalent towards it. I had so much I wanted to express and longed for an outlet.

The apprenticeship stretched over two years. In the final stage, the student applied for a journeyman certificate, an intricate process in itself. Once the certificate was received, the apprentice became a practitioner in their own right: a fully qualified men's tailor. I found that it wasn't mastering advanced skills that drove my studies but rather gaining a hands-on technical understanding. I realised that once I had understood how to construct, I could experiment more freely within the creative process. When I understood the difference between a tailored-made men's jacket and the one you would buy on the high street, it seemed time to move on.

Tailoring and my small hometown seemed a suffocating combination. At nineteen, it was not professional skill I was searching for, but personal liberation. I longed for a new, yet-to-be-experienced form of self-expression, to leave the homogeneous place of my hometown and the creatively limited space that traditional tailoring had proved to be.

London became a place of refuge. Once in the big city, I started an internship, working for a fashion designer who designed both garments and cloth. At this point, I still assumed fashion was the medium to which I wanted to apply my new-found knowledge.

When I first arrived in London, I felt its energy holding the promise of acceptance. The possibilities for self-expression felt endless. Its sense of freedom has coloured my relationship with the city. London allowed me to meet other 'Fadhels' and to experience kinship while discovering new sides of myself. Gone were the norms of the socially homogeneous Sjuhärad and the previously felt limitations in how I could express myself.

During the internship, the approach to making felt equally as unknown, vast, and liberating as London itself. The studio I worked for collected craft-based techniques from everywhere and remixed them into something greater. My first introduction to weaving was within this, for me, context of newness. I learnt that weaving involves much invisible labour before the making is even commenced, so much is carried out in the preparatory process. Even within this experimental mode of making, the loom required such care, rigour, and control. Yet, once the preparatory work was completed, once finally weaving, freedom presented itself. I was given a cotton yarn dyed in the next-door kitchen, which also doubled as a warp winding space (the process of preparing the yarn to be put on the loom). I wove a denim fabric, turned into a pair of jeans and an accompanying jacket. My previous regimented studies helped my ability to manoeuvre the experimental way of making.

This short period had a huge influence on me.

In London, I was simultaneously introduced to the many steps of the loom as I experienced how the many internal iterations of my own identity gained outward expressions. Weaving became synonymous with this sense of freedom. During this period of exposure and exploration I understood weaving was the medium I should be working through.

Going backwards in the process, from designing a garment to its construction to arriving at the making of cloth, finally connected the dots for me.

In the city of new-found self-expression, kinship and creative venture, I could finally connect my innate desire to understand the 'how-to's' of making with the desire to express myself and see them merge into one process. It all made sense on the loom. Using one's hands in the continuous motion of letting the weft go through the warp, allowed for the creation of a potentially infinite amount of structures.

In this remixed state of making, I understood that weaving was not something binary but plural.

Just as there are countless patterned cloths to be woven on the loom, so too are the intricate, varied, and numerous cultural expressions to be captured within the cloth itself.

***

In London, the scope of the English language was broad, both in terms of domestic dialects and international accents. When speaking, my Swedish accent made itself known in no time, yet it was spoken among a sea of other international accents. Sweden is often perceived as a place of cultural excellence abroad, a strong welfare state known for its tall, beautiful, well-travelled and well-dressed people—not to mention the paid paternity leave(!)

In London, I only needed to embrace the melodic residues of Västgötska in my English for the familiar perceptions of my name, as experienced in Sweden, to be perceived in a different light—due to my Swedish roots.

I had a peculiar name, but I spoke in a familiar accent. Due to my accent, despite my name, I garnered a new sense of acceptance. I suppose the origin of my name, together with my accent, just added another layer of perceived exoticness in the rigid minds of the British.

In London, I was a foreigner, my identity was to be a native Swede. I didn't try to be perceived as Swedish, I simply was. Unlike in Sweden, where I repeatedly felt the need to try and prove my native identity. The feeling of being the rightful owner of 'Swedishness' was an entirely new experience.

When I eventually moved to the UK permanently, I reflected on my father's navigation of Swedish culture as an immigrant. I later became a mere international art student in the city. I had the privilege of getting an education and searching for freedom, all while having the Swedish state pay for my travel, tuition fee, and monthly stipend. My experience of journeying is a complete '180' from my father's.

Today, I have lived in London for nearly a decade. I spend most of my days speaking, reading, writing and even daydreaming in English. Even this text is written in my new primary but second language. Although prejudices persist, they occur within a place of perceived freedom: the fast-paced, vast surroundings of the metropolis itself.

***

Much like finding my craft, embracing my queerness has also been a non-linear journey in and of itself. As I eventually approached the basket, the lessons of my past regimented studies and previous experiences of what tradition could be had become clearer: to find that sought-after place of belonging in my identity, I found I had to make up with tradition.

Before being introduced to weaving, I had approached and rejected traditional mediums as my own, yet I sought to return to them. Weaving is equal to tailoring in its regimented process. It requires control. Only, its absolute way of doing aligns with my inherent attraction to craft, as it balances rigorous process with room for self-expression.

From an early age, I expressed my sense of individuality and often suffered the consequences of claiming space, and owning the parts of myself that clearly distinguished me from the norm, as others imposed their opinion on my way of being. I deviated from the norm in both how I presented myself and in the ways I conveyed my view of the world around me.

I now understand that being queer, much like being in between two cultures, has enabled me to observe and understand the world around me more objectively.

As a Swede with a North African background, already navigating Västgötska and Förortssvenska, being queer has added another layer of sensibility to the already complex social awareness that comes with being mixed—an ability that has enabled me to further pick up, decipher and act on subtle nuances in social cues, language or behaviours—in order to fit in. Moreover, being queer has given me a greater objective understanding towards the reasons for various cultural practices to form, both in Sweden and beyond. This added layer of comprehension continues to inform my perception of the social frameworks in which my two cultures operate.

It has helped me to understand how social stigma develops and how social hierarchies are not only formed but kept in place, or how prejudice towards the queer community is prevalent in both spaces. I have found this to be a 'silent' type of knowledge, one that is only understood by peers: other queer people with 'Mourali-clinging' names. Needless to say at this point: my perception of the world was moulded by growing up in an average Swedish working-class, heteronormative household (despite my shared Tunisian heritage and queer identity). Finding weaving parallels my journey of embracing my queerness, as I discovered it to be a medium that holds a multitude of expressions.

Weaving enabled me, through material and technique, to use its process as an outlet to tell my own stories: it allowed me to be in keeping with tradition, whilst subverting it at the same time. As the narrator of this publication, my storytelling found its voice from being rooted in the labour-intensive process of weaving. The written narrations of the basket, alongside weaving, have allowed for a personal erosion of the internalised tensions between my queer identity and the traditional spaces of both my cultures. Whilst on the loom, I could make up with tradition and find my haven by honing in on everything I perceived to reject me.

As narrator, I could, in print, combine the certainty of words, the absolute elements of craft and the previously foreign elements of tradition. Instead of the felt tensions between my cultures and queer identity being put against each other, they could merge as part of this storytelling. Much like how Lennart found pride in his practice in his later years, I now find a similar pride in embodying the histories of my dual heritage whilst fully embracing being part of its future legacy.

Today, I understand my own queer resistance and its source. I find it in my very existence, in my ability to manoeuvre across cultural perspectives and worlds—it is the desire to understand perspectives and connections that exist in the unarticulated, the unspoken, but the lived.

NOTES

1. Carpenter, W. H., quoted in Salomon, O. (1888) *The Slöjd in the Service of the School*. Translated by W. H. Carpenter. New York: Industrial Education Association, preface.
2. ISOF—The Institute for Language and Folklore (2021) *Götamål*. https://www.isof.se/dialekter/lar-dig-mer-om-svenska-dialekter/utforska-svenska-dialekter/gotamal [20/05/2024].
3. The Institute for Language and Folklore (ISOF) is a Swedish government authority responsible for building, collecting, and disseminating knowledge about Sweden's languages and culture.

   In correspondence with the Institute, the following inputs were given about Västgötska:

   * Referring to Götaskorrning as a 'rolling r' can be misleading, as 'rolling' typically refers to tongue-tip r's. In this case, it concerns a tongue-rooted 'r', which is difficult to translate. Perhaps it might be best to describe it as being pronounced 'with the back of the tongue'?
   * *korg* (basket) is [kɔrj] in standard Swedish. In traditional Västgötska, it most likely becomes *kôrj* [kərj], though this is not certain.
   * *Hedared* is most likely [ˈheːdaˌreːd]. In dialect, might be [ˈheːaˌʁeː] with a back (tongue-rooted) 'r', although the specific dialectal pronunciation cannot be confirmed.
   * The tj-sound in *kyrka* (church) is usually written as [ɕ]. The dialectal *körka* should be [ɕørka].
   * *Hedareds stavkyrka* (Hedared stave church) [ˈheːdaˌreːds ˈstɑːvˌɕyrka].

4. Johansson, A.O., Sandhults hembygdsförening (1954) *Sandhult: Gammalt och Nytt*. Borås: Kliché & Litografiska AB, p. 156.
5. ISOF—The Institute for Language and Folklore (2021) *Götamål*. https://www.isof.se/dialekter/lar-dig-mer-om-svenska-dialekter/utforska-svenska-dialekter/gotamal [20/05/2024].
6. Wasling L., Wasling M. (2020) *Stadsdelar i Borås*. Borås: Exakta Print, pp. 205–208.
7. Boverket—The Swedish National Board of Housing, Building and Planning (2020) *Under miljonprogrammet byggdes en miljon bostäder: Miljonprogrammet som uttryck*. https://www.boverket.se/sv/samhallsplanering/stadsutveckling/miljonprogrammet/ [2024/06/08]. Translated by the author.
8. Ibid.
9. Boverket—The Swedish National Board of Housing, Building and Planning (2020) *Under miljonprogrammet byggdes en miljon bostäder: Fler låga hus än höghus*. https://www.boverket.se/sv/samhallsplanering/stadsutveckling/miljonprogrammet/ [2024/06/08]. Translated by the author.
10. Boverket—The Swedish National Board of Housing, Building and Planning (2020) *Under miljonprogrammet byggdes en miljon bostäder: Miljonprogrammet fick tidigt kritik*. https://www.boverket.se/sv/samhallsplanering/stadsutveckling/miljonprogrammet/ [2024/06/08]. Translated by the author.
11. Boverket—The Swedish National Board of Housing, Building and Planning (2020) *Under miljonprogrammet byggdes en miljon bostäder: Dags att renovera husen*. https://www.boverket.se/sv/samhallsplanering/stadsutveckling/miljonprogrammet/ [2024/06/08]. Translated by the author.
12. Hjelm, F. (2008) *Historien om Borås stadsbebyggelse ll: Om Hus och människor*. Borås: Dahlins Tryckeri AB, p. 7. Translated by the author.
13. Ibid., p. 42.
14. Ibid.
15. Ibid., p. 43. Translated by the author.
16. Ibid. Translated by the author.
17. Ibid., p. 92. Translated by the author.
18. Ibid., p. 96. Translated by the author.
19. Polismyndigheten (2023). *Lägesbild över utsatta områden*. Stockholm: Polismyndigheten, p. 40.
20. Polismyndigheten (2024) *Utsatta områden*. https://polisen.se/om-polisen/polisens-arbete/utsatta-omraden/ [04/06/2024]. Translated by the author.
21. Ibid.
22. Polismyndigheten (2023). *Lägesbild över utsatta områden*. Stockholm: Polismyndigheten, p. 9.

23. Polismyndigheten (2024) *Utsatta områden*.
    https://polisen.se/om-polisen/polisens-arbete/utsatta-omraden/ [04/06/2024].
    Translated by the author.
24. Lagerström, S. H. G. (2004) *Månsing: knallarnas hemliga språk*. Borås: Junito Förlag, p. 8.
    Translated by the author.
25. Ibid.
26. SAOB—Svenska Akademiens Ordböcker (2024) *Månsing*.
    https://svenska.se/saob/?sok=månsing&pz=1 [01/07/2024].
27. Lagerström (2004), p. 8. Translated by the author.
28. Ibid., pp. 20–58. Translated by the author.
26. Ibid. Translated by the author.
27. Ibid., p. 7.
28. Ibid., p. 1.
29. Nationalencyklopedin (n.d.) *Skilling*.
    https://www.ne.se/uppslagsverk/encyklopedi/lång/skilling-(myntenhet-i-sverige)[01/07/2024].
    Translated by the author.
30. Lagerström (2004), p. 7.
31. Ibid., p. 16. Translated by the author.
32. Ljungström (1865), cited in Lagerström (2004), p. 16. Translated by the author.
33. ISOF—The Institute for Language and Folklore (2024) *Förortssvenska*.
    https://www.isof.se/svenska-spraket/lar-dig-mer-om-svenska-spraket/forortssvenska
    [20/05/2024]. Translated by the author.
34. Ibid. Translated by the author.
35. ISOF—The Institute for Language and Folklore (2021) 'Svensk ordföljd som symbol',
    Språkrådsbloggen, 2 November.
    https://www.isof.se/svenska-spraket/pa-gang/sprakradsbloggen/inlagg/2021-11-02-svensk-
    ordfoljd-som-symbol [20/05/2024]. Translated by the author.
36. Ibid. Translated by the author.
37. ISOF—The Institute for Language and Folklore (2024) *Förortssvenska*.
    https://www.isof.se/svenska-spraket/lar-dig-mer-om-svenska-spraket/forortssvenska
    [20/05/2024]. Translated by the author.
38. Ibid. Translated by the author.
39. Agrell, B. (2019) *Maria Sandel och folkbildningen. Inte bara vett och vetande—bildningens
    betydelse i Maria Sandels författarskap*. Stockholm: Maria Sandelsällskapet, p. 62.
    https://urn.kb.se/resolve?urn=urn:nbn:se:lb-lbq2zx14lsnksnsmc5-faksimil [01/07/2024]
40. ISOF—The Institute for Language and Folklore [2024] *Förortssvenska*.
    https://www.isof.se/svenska-spraket/lar-dig-mer-om-svenska-spraket/forortssvenska
    [20/05/2024]. Translated by the author.
41. SAOB—Svenska Akademiens Ordböcker (2024) *Lagom*.
    https://svenska.se/saob/?sok=lagom&pz=2 [15/07/2024]. Translated by the author.
42. Ibid. Translated by the author.

IMAGE CREDITS

Unless specified, all images were taken by the author in 2013 or 2018, or sourced from the author's personal photo albums. In the latter case, the dates and the photographer's identity are unknown.

Upcoming pp. 59–78 (from the left):

9. Screenshot, Google Maps (2024).
18. Screenshot, Google Translate (2024).

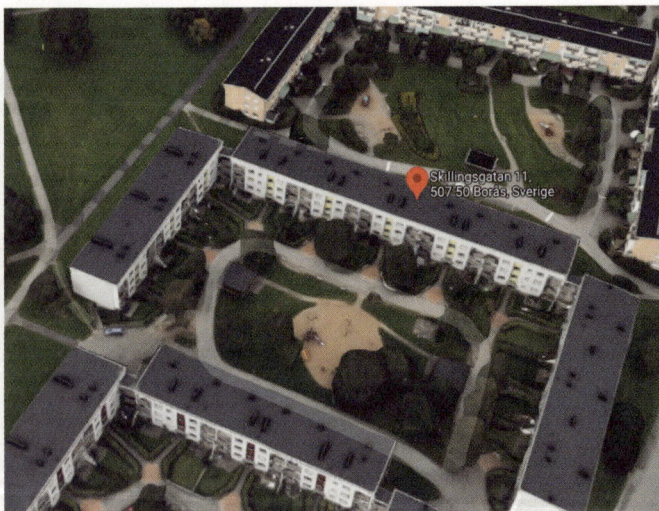

Skillingsgatan 11,
507 50 Borås, Sverige

67

lagom är bäst

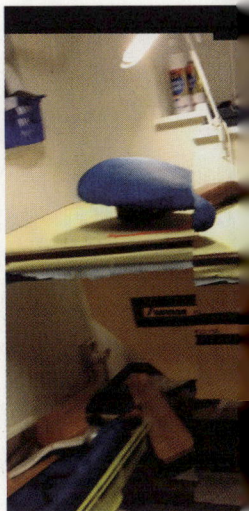

Engelska

everything in
moderation

Öppna i Google Översätt · Feedback

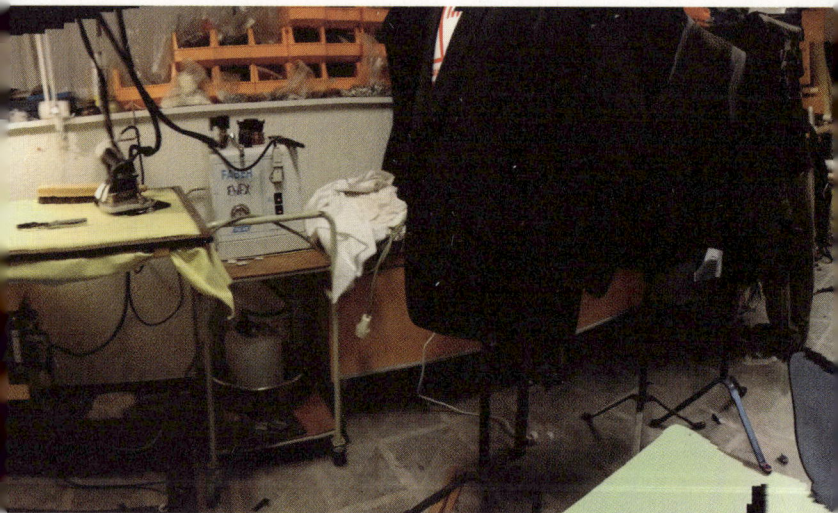

City&Guilds
of London
Art School

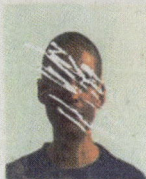

Fadhel
Mourali
Course: Foundation Diplom
MOUF2310_A0111617
DOB: 23/10/93
Card Expiry Date: 22/05/2017

This card is not transferable and remains the property of City & Guilds of
Art School Ltd. If found please contact us on 0207 735 2306

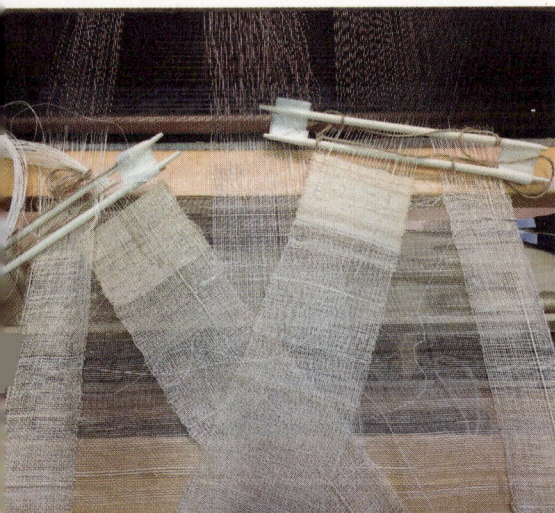

ON QUEERNESS AND CRAFT

IN CONVERSATION WITH RAISA KABIR

Fadhel: [00:00:25] To quickly reintroduce the project: it can be described as a patchwork consisting of various moving parts that together form a whole. My ambition has been to use storytelling and 'patch' together heritage, identity and cultural belonging with craft in the centre. I have strived to do that by mirroring my Swedish great-grandfather's craft practice to my own, and exploring our family's cultural evolution. My queer identity has played a huge part in that. So, our conversation aims to deepen the reader's understanding of queerness and highlight it in all its forms from your point of view and practice.

My first question: How does your queer identity intersect with your artistic practice?

Raisa: [00:01:27] As you know, having these multiple identities, sometimes I think at first glance, people maybe don't notice that my work is queer. When I was at Chelsea [College of Arts], and doing my final undergraduate show, the kind of central search, and the central research that I embarked on, was a kind of intertwining. I was researching the identities of South Asian, queer, LGBTQ women, and their position in London, in the UK—looking at the diaspora especially. I interwove that research with ideas about visibility, and language—looking at queer people of colour, and how one starts to be read as queer, and how that is intertwined with dress, location, and space. How it was assumed that if you were South Asian, even if you were queer-presenting or even femme-presenting, that your queerness could be erased. The assumption would be that if someone had a global background—one that wasn't considered Western, European, or white—someone was straight.

That body of work was called *Lift The Veil and See Our Silent Language*. The work was woven using textile symbols and practices related to Bangladesh, such as

Jamdani techniques, South Asian weaving, silk and cotton weaving. At first glance, perhaps if you didn't know anything about textile history, you would just presume it was a beautiful piece of cloth, not to blow my own trumpet or anything... The idea that it's just a decorative, silk-patterned cloth and that beneath the surface there isn't anything under that. But in actuality, it was a kind of patterning and reforming of Bengali script, *Bangla*. The patterns were actually hidden and encoded letters, and then parts were highlighted, so if you could read Bengali, you would be able to read the poem I'd woven into the cloth.

If someone could read Bengali, they'd be able to read the kind of queerness and the politics encoded within the cloth and not just see it at face value. Instead, being able to read each other's small codes, if someone is wearing a shawl or a sari: those sartorial and cultural cues are also queered. So [through these codes] you can actually see like, that this isn't someone that's just, you know, [dressed for] an 'auntie function'. In actuality, this is someone who... I don't know what the right word is, I don't want to say subversive, or mean to say deviate, not deviant per se, but someone who deviates from those cultural dress norms; if you can speak each other's 'language', through these codes, then you can read [and understand] each other. It's the same kind of practice with other South Asians across the diaspora; people from Pakistan, Afghanistan, India, Sri Lanka, that kind of surrounding area, would have similar ways of seeing other people's codes of dress and queerness in each other.

That was one of the first times [my queerness] really intersected with my practice quite explicitly. People had to read the text label about it [to understand it completely], but I accompanied [the woven work] with a sound piece.

So, even if you didn't know it was a poem, you could listen to the poem and then that would alert you to the fact that this is not just a cloth, it's actually a text. This was when I started to combine these things together; it's not just about referencing South Asian identity, but showing that South Asia has a long history of textile practice, heritage, influence, and exchange with the Western world.

Another direct element of the work also included a series of photographs. I interviewed other South Asian women, trans-, bi-queer and gender non-conforming people (back then, it wasn't called non-binary). I took photographs of them and created a montage series. I asked people questions about where they felt like they truly belonged, and if it was a real space or an imaginary space. How do their clothes fit? Do they feel comfortable in queer spaces in London? Did they feel comfortable in private or public spaces, and the felt difference when presenting as queer in South Asian cultural community spaces, such as mosques or familial spaces.

We asked people: Where would you imagine yourself to feel the most comfortable? Then we would together recreate those imagined spaces [for the photographs], if they didn't already exist. For example, we went to the first mosque that was ever built in the UK... I had lesbian-identifying people saying: *I don't want to wear feminine clothing because I wear clothing this way, but I also still like to highlight this part of my identity*. We wanted to make sure people felt as comfortable as they could in these photos.

I would say that since that project, every part of my work has a queer element, which also comes through with its direct politics. I think that is probably the largest aspect, because sometimes we just assume that everyone who makes political work is political, and not everyone who is queer, or LGBTQ, or part of a global diaspora, will be political.

But often you will find that the people who delve deeper into their practice and find a sort of deeper perspective, that has a political focus, that could be as broad or as narrow as you can describe, tend to have a kind of 'queer background'. I think maybe that is where that extra subtle layer is, where, yes, I'm not just talking about diaspora, I'm not just talking about colonialism: I'm also talking about specific nuances. For example, a lot of my work criticises and brings into focus the ways in which the Bangladeshi state is oppressive to minorities, ethnic tribal peoples.

[The perspective] becomes more complicated, nu-anced, more kind of globally outward-looking, where you can see, I have solidarity with a lot of my Bengali, Bangladeshi queer folk—artists, designers, textile workers who are, I wouldn't say suffering, but just having to exist under the hangover of the [punity] law which is still in place in Bangladesh, the 377, where being queer is punishable by death. It's still there and even though people say there is a large trans, Hijra community or there's, you know, I have a lot of people who are part of this very healthy, wonderful community but they do have to be careful.
These communities do exist, but they have to operate within what is current law at the moment. Often people who have freedom of movement are people from slightly more comfortable middle-class backgrounds. It's a completely different story if you're working-class. So, it's those nuances that appear when you look at class etc. I'm not going to speak for all queer people, but this is the case specifically for me, in my practice, and how my queerness [manifests as part of it].

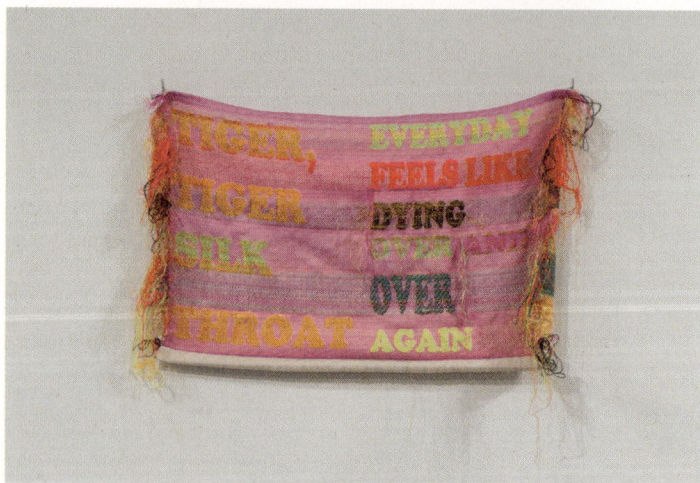

Everyday Feels like Dying, Over and Over and Over Again... (2024).
Photo: Mike Mosher.

Everyday Feels like Dying, Over and Over and Over Again... (2024).
Photo: Mike Mosher.

I know a lot of people, South Asians, that maybe come to the UK, who aren't queer, but are often from quite wealthy backgrounds, and come to the UK or the US and have little reflection on their dominant caste position for example... Having 'the queerness' [in such a context] I think allows people to be more critical of their own positionality, and ask: Where do I fit in? Where do I hold power? How does my work and politics actually extend, and how do I use my position to point out and draw attention to these wider, more connected political struggles—the Bangladeshi state's occupation, and military sequestering of Rangamati Chittagong Hill Tracts. This is not really spoken about by anyone in Bangladesh, apart from people who are artists, people who are political, people who are leftists, and people who have that queer sensibility.

When you are marginalised, say under the state of Bangladesh, you have no option but to be political. I would say in the UK, the US or in Europe, people are losing some of that. You come across this homo-nationalism or even homonormativity where a lot of people just take [their freedom of expression] for granted. There are probably some places where gay, queer, and LGBTQ people [due to their wealth and other privileges] have less urgency and see less of a need for the kind of political movements that we saw in the 60s and 70s, where everyone was united. This is coming under threat and hard-won rights are easily taken away.

We can see some of that intersectional politics come into play, where certain people of different [queer, LGBTQ+] identities may not be fully ready to question their position, their privilege and their political stance, or take their position and freedoms for granted. I'm not saying that is everything, but it's these deeper nuances, and, you know, I don't put on my Instagram that I'm queer because I work a lot in Bangladesh. I can't take the chance that someone might see that at some point. I'm quite lucky, because apparently there are lots of Raisa Kabirs in Bangladesh, it's very hard to find me, but you know, I work there, I have to maintain lots of professional relationships. So that's another thing where I can't just put that out. It's obviously in my work, and I'll say it in texts and things, but I can't just put it in my bio, even though I'd love to, I cannot.

The other aspect is the work that I made, that got commissioned by the Ford Foundation in New York, that was very specifically about disability. It was very much about the care networks that marginalised folks, who are LGBT, queer, migrants, disabled or sick have created to support those who need care when they are let down by state systems, and how these [kind of care networks] are usually found within marginalised groups, and became much more popularised and public during the pandemic.

Fadhel: [00:13:47] So, so many great things mentioned, but speaking of, or going back to care—being in the UK, Bangladesh, you're in America right now... I want to know more about community.

Can you elaborate on the role of community and collaboration within your practice?

Raisa: [00:14:13] I haven't talked about my graduate project for a really long time, but that was the first time that I did see [my work] as a collaboration. I didn't see it as me researching these people in my community, I was like: *No, we're going to make artwork together. Tell me, what is it that you see? Do you see yourself?* It was the first time I was really centring collaboration. Skipping ahead to 2020, to a work called the *House Made of Tin (a socially distanced weaving performance),* which is a reference to the description of my dad's house when he was growing up. I never visited it, but it was a house made of tin, and it was tethered, like a tent, to the ground. It was very precarious. The work was a comment on precarity, about how so many of us are living in these precarious states, and actually completely rely on those kinds of care networks; the collaboration [of care] and seeing ourselves as doing things for the good of the community.

So this work was commissioned by the Ford Foundation Gallery in New York and was a whole series on disability, and [the collaborators/curators in the project] were mainly coming at it from a US context, but artists were from all over there and Europe included. I spent most of my fee paying, commissioning, queer artists, performers, people who were disabled performers, disabled POC performers, to work with me on building this woven structure.

That's [a context] I've always kind of worked in. Very early on, I was part of a collective called Collective Creativity. It was a QTBIPOC arts collective, with Raju Rage, Evan Ifekoya and Rudy Loewe in London. When we first all graduated, we found that we were kind of 'recovering' from the UK institutional academy, the academic system. Working together to create space with each other, creating these kinds of commissions, going into different schools, it was a very beautiful way to build sustainability and sustenance. Not just the sharing, but the kind of co-creation that happens when you build a foundation together.

We made a publication about how to survive art school as queer POCs, but there were also lots of other facets. Being in London, its art world, working out how we could navigate these systems or these institutional structures that weren't really ever made for us as queer and trans artists of colour. We built a community of support and resources in London.

The kind of catalyst framework of how to make it as an artist is this very weird individualist concept of genius artist, and actually what we noticed when looking at the histories of artist collectives in the 80s and 90s, is that you actually have to create community, and not just like in a wishy washy way, but create structural spaces—spaces for conversation. We would not just talk to our peers of a similar age, but with people who were in their forties, fifties, sixties. This was crucial. We found that the most beneficial thing was to talk to people, interview people and talk to our elders. Art elders, people who would have been doing political work in the 80s and 90s. That connected us to a much wider legacy.

We would always share, not just education, but resources, and I think that was one of the biggest things. If you have access to resources in any way, and if parts of your community perhaps didn't have the luxury of going to university, what we would do is we go to archives, we would take resources, we would put things out. We would share, open doors, carve out spaces for our community and to make that kind of, not bridge, but to sort of bash open the door a bit, edge our way in, and create spaces on our own terms. I could go on and on, but the queer community in London was a very beautiful thing. I've also worked in Bangladesh, with queer artists and designers. If you find your people, you will see the spaces for each other and share [those spaces].

the structure, collectively woven, connecting us all.

House Made of Tin (a socially distanced weaving performance) (2020).
Film Still: Raisa Kabir.

Fadhel: [00:20:16] Going back to community and your Bangladeshi heritage, can you speak on the importance of intergenerational knowledge within your family or community? Has that played a part in your work?

Raisa: [00:20:33] In terms of?

Fadhel: [00:20:36] In this project, I've worked with people in the village where my great-grandfather grew up, I have worked with museum archivist(s), and the local residents, to essentially [for me] explore 'Swedishness' in a way that I've never experienced before... It gave me a new understanding of the lived experience of my own roots. I have been exposed to the knowledge that we've had in the family; of the land, of the craft, and that has helped me to look at my own identity in a new way, and made me understand my work in a new way.

Have you had a similar experience working with Bangladeshi practitioners? Kind of, looking back to be able to look forward?

Raisa: [00:21:22] I remember one of the most beautiful synchronicities... [in the beginning], before I even got a chance to work as a weaver, as an artist in Bangladesh... When I was writing my dissertation on South Asian queer identity, and the tutors at university were like:

We have nothing to tell you,

It looks like you're doing fine, you are doing really well,

We don't actually have any knowledge [about these topics], this is a distinction, this is an 'A', just go forth.

I was like, *No feedback, no nothing?*

I remember the first time meeting Bangladeshi queer academics who were working at UAL, at London College of Fashion. One [of them] was just a little bit older, maybe ten years older than me, doing their PhD, and they were like: *Give me your dissertation, I'll read it,* and they just gave the best feedback. That was the first moment of me connecting to other Bangladeshi, queer-identifying people, people who were working in fashion and textiles but were also a part of London, and specifically understood the Bangladeshi diaspora. I'm living in London, I'm from Manchester; there's a specificity there. I think that was really the first experience of being like: *Oh, someone else gets it.*

Later on, Lipi [Begum, the tutor who read Raisa's dissertation] would work with the Muslin Trust, which set up this exhibition and research festival—the 2016 Muslin Festival in partnership with Drik Gallery in Dhaka. That's when I travelled there and I got to work with Bangladeshi Jamdani weavers, and Adivasi Indigenous textile and fashion designer Tenzing Chakma. I think it's so hard to frame... some of the liminality between us because it's like, yes, we're queer, but also we're working with textiles, as artists, there are many layers on top of layers here. There is a shared rapport, a shared connection, but it's never really explicitly expressed.

I think that's what I'm always trying to get at, it's not just that I'm queer or South Asian—it's a particular experience. These factors together create a very specific sensibility... We ended up talking about oppression, sharing about the kind of real pressing culture politics; people's survival, their human rights, and the importance of preserving Chakma weaving. There's also a lot of complexity in how this craft is valued, especially

when compared to Bangladesh's national crafts.
Many subtle, underlying factors come into play.

Fadhel: [00:24:39] I want to touch upon tensions. In my
own heritage, my father is Tunisian and mother is Swedish...
Opening up a conversation about queerness, as you
mentioned, can be filled with taboos, it's often hard to do,
and can be a 'no-go zone'. You mentioned it briefly, but
how have you, or have you, encountered tensions between
honouring your cultural heritage whilst embracing non-
conforming identities?

Where do you see, or where have you experienced such
tensions?

Raisa: [00:25:25] I think... I haven't found any
tensions... I think especially when I've worked [in a
place like] New York, and then met loads of South
Asian, queer-identifying people, and I'm talking
about my textiles, there's been like the most beautiful
synchronisation. I've also worked in Limehouse [in
East London] with South Asian, Muslim, Bangladeshi
communities, lovely women. You know, especially,
at times when I had like half a shaved head, and things
like that, people are just very accepting. I have never
really sort of explicitly mentioned it, but personally,
I'm a chameleon. I'm someone that can get on with
anyone. But also, I'm cis, I'm very femme-presenting,
if people want to ignore a certain side of me, they can.
But I have encountered [in Limehouse] very sweet
people, who have been like: *I really like your undercut*.

OK, here's another thing: later on, when I would work
with [members of] the Bangladeshi community, lovely
Muslims, Hijabis, who work with sewing and weaving,
we did beautiful weaving workshops and had an
amazing time... I think when I was a lot younger,
I would say there was maybe a trepidation there,

before I'd gone to Bangladesh, and before I'd felt accepted by my community. I think that is probably very early on... [which was] probably what led me to doing that research as an undergraduate.

I think the tension came from myself. I would now probably identify that as internalised racism. We think that we won't be accepted. We are already anticipating rejection because we are actually internalising very racist ideas about homophobic communities.

And yes, that's probably something that gets told to the Muslim community, [that it] will be really homophobic and won't accept you [as queer]. But actually, you know, you as a person, when you finally do work with people and with communities, they aren't going to behave in that way. I think it is an internalised misconception where we stay away from our communities because we think we're going to be rejected. We [as queer people] think that there is no common ground, and in fact there is so much common ground.

There's so much more there than one facet to your identity. It is because of being queer, that I have been able to expand upon those politics, where I've been able to work with [someone like] the Bangladeshi designer Tenzing Chakma, and understand the very complex geopolitical border histories.

But getting back to the Bangladeshi community in London... The tension, I think a lot of was internal and also came from religion. I've seen it in my other peers as well, who maybe don't work in textiles, who really felt like they couldn't engage with their faith and almost felt disowned. We felt like we had to go the other way, I covered it in my dissertation as well, it's like: *I'm just going to be in white queer spaces, dancing and all that kind of thing*.

I've seen it in other peers and in myself. I went to a queer Muslim women's group in 2012 and that was really beautiful, meeting other queer Muslim women, the queer Muslim community, people who were from the Inclusive Mosque Initiative. It was as inclusive as possible, so there were people from lots of different denominations. And that healed a lot of internalised tensions between Muslim, South Asian and Queer identities.

So, I think the tension is usually within yourself, as soon as you make connections with people in your own community, it will allow you to go and make connections with the Muslim community, who are not queer at all, but you're not going to be rejected, there will be a lot of common ground here. There is so much to grow and share from, and to not feel like you have to lose a whole part of yourself [because of your queer identity].

Fadhel: [00:30:28] If we flip the question—in more white, heteronormative spaces, as a person of colour, who's queer, who has this multicultural background, is there a navigation that you have to do there?

You mentioned tensions being sort of internalised, as a queer person in brown or Muslim spaces, is there a similar 'tension' to navigate in a predominantly white space, in academia or art?

Raisa: [00:31:39] I would say that being at Chelsea [College of Arts] was really hard, being part of that institution, but that was also to do with being from Manchester, not having gone to boarding school, not being from a very rich background... Just these very cultural things, but also being brown, being queer as well. Entering into some of these institutions with all these identities, as you say, was, specifically

94

for me, being disabled and having a chronic illness, navigating support was really hard, but the head of the department was always very supportive and that did help in the end... What I will say is, academia is not for everyone, it is built to exclude and naturally that is a painful process to be in, being brown, being queer, trying to get through art school, having bad mental health or other chronic, physical disabilities. All of that combined doesn't give you the best stepping stone to exist within these structures, within these institutions.

Not just in academia, also in art spaces, with imposter syndrome, where people who are very qualified, very good in their work, don't feel like they see themselves represented in any way so ultimately feel others are better qualified than them. I can definitely identify with that. I don't think I saw any, or many, Muslim weavers or people who were queer and brown or doing anything in the UK at that point. You know, ten years ago, it was a very different time. There was little discourse on racial awareness that had entered the mainstream. The landscape of curriculum, academia, the political landscape, the queer landscape, everything was very different...

It took me a really long time to even consider going into postgraduate study. I was like, I can't go back into *that* space, unless it's completely right, and this is why I ended up coming to Chicago [SAIC], because most of the department is queer and trans. There is a political thread; it's part of the curriculum, it's part of everything, the classes, the teaching and spaces are shared and set up for [this common ground]. Particularly coming from textile teaching in Europe and in the UK, where we're very aligned to straight women, straight white women, who work in museums. It's a very narrow point of view. Obviously, there are amazing scholars and amazing people within that. I've met some incredible people.

I've also met some really terrible people. I remember taking my undergraduate graduate collection and trying to see if I could do an MA somewhere, with someone [an institution] who would get my politics, someone that would understand my nuances. I never thought that the RCA [Royal College of Art] would accept me, so I never applied. I ended up taking my graduate collection to show the head of textiles at a college to discuss MAs. The professor took one look at my collection and she got so excited, she was like:

This is really exquisite, this is really, like, high level. Oh, I love this, this is amazing.

When I was telling her what the work was about, I was telling her about my grandma or something about this work about *Purdah*, which is the veil, and then she turned to me and she goes:
Raisa, are you Muslim?
I was like: Yes?
Oh, but you don't wear the veil?
I was like: No...
Then, you know, as she was hearing about the work, she was just like:
Raisa, are you a lesbian?
And I was like: No, I'm not... I'm queer...
I don't remember what I said, it was just a really weird question. She's like:
Oh, it just doesn't look like you are,
and I was just like:
Wow, okay, I'm out of here.

But she got so excited. She was like: *Oh, we'll make such good work, it would be amazing if you came here.*

She got very excited about the fact that I was queer, that I was Muslim and that I was a weaver, and it was very uncomfortable.

Fadhel: [00:37:07] Token.

Raisa: [00:37:08] Yes, really tokenistic, really objectifying, you know, all these horrible things that I never thought would be part of my work. That someone would see it like that, so I'll just say that about tensions, and those [kinds of] spaces, you know, it really put me off. You know, she's a professor, she's got a PhD and she's talking to me like this...

Fadhel: [00:37:34] So, keeping within academia, going into theory, my experience with universities is that, all these perspectives that we just mentioned, are often overlooked in favour of some grand theory. For me, this whole project is about the lived experience. I have found that the lived experience is often not acknowledged as a true form of knowledge without some sort of intellectualisation.

When you make work, how do you avoid the discourse around it becoming too abstract or too academic? Do you think the tangibility of craft helps to make it easier to communicate, rather than just putting notes onto paper?

Raisa: [00:38:43] I did find a place within academia, on an academic MA, and it was fine but then the pandemic happened and I left... What I will say is, something I really struggled with... I would write, you know, I did thrive a lot with the writing of things, but the feedback would be: *This needs to be cited*, and I was like, well, this is my experience. This is the experience of everyone I know, no one's written about it yet, it can't be cited. I'm talking about craft. I'm talking about embodied knowledge, things that are passed down through the body. This is an archive.

97

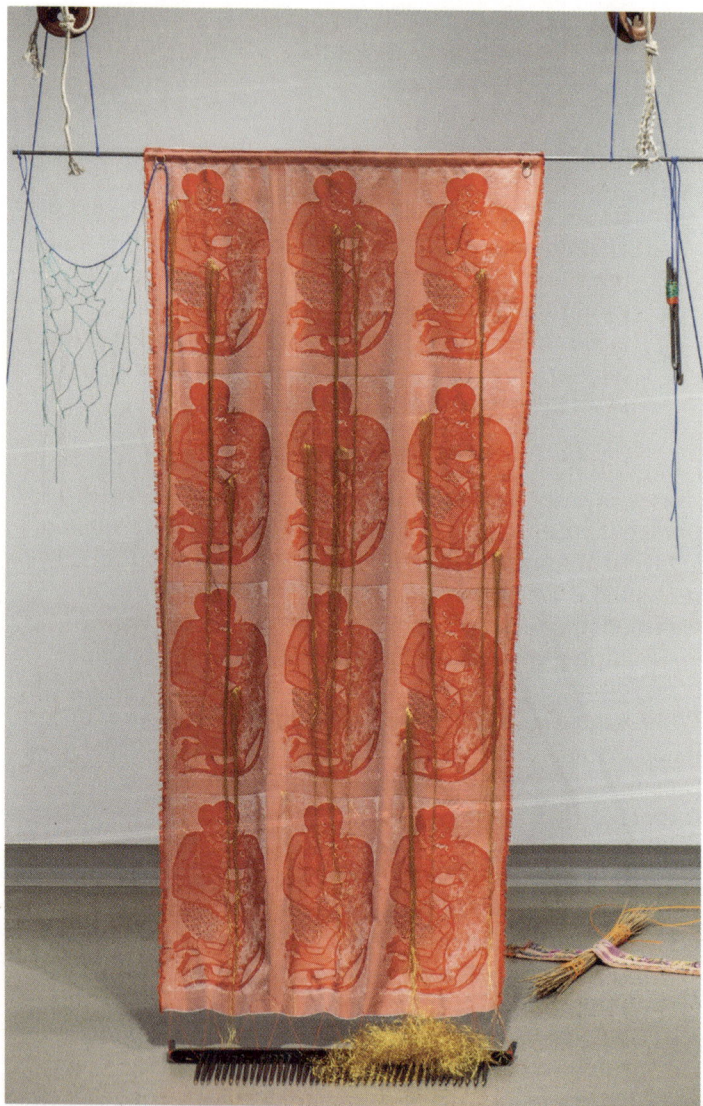

Tiger, Tiger... Silk Throat (2023). Photo: Mike Mosher.

I really came up against that a lot. I struggled with academia after a while because I was like, actually, I don't want to spend all that time creating beautiful connections with Indigenous communities and weavers, then for that to be reduced to academic research in a paper. I don't want to be this researcher. I don't want to have this beautiful connection with the families and communities that I was working with, and then for them, for their lives, to be reduced to research. That's not what I wanted. I was like, that's not my aim here. My aim here is to honour embodied archives and not archives in that specific sense, but in the fact that specific knowledge that's held in the body, that is shared in these very specific ways, is just as valid, because we know it's true. We know this is knowledge, we know it is handed down, we know it is verified, and certified, especially when talking about craft, geopolitics and oral history.

I would mention some things around history, and my tutor would say: *Where is that cited?* I would be like: *It's my life.* Through my parents, they left Bangladesh, they lived through partition. It's our life. This is us. A lot of the time, things are cited because [researchers] interviewed people. People do value the fact that if you interview people, that is knowledge. So it should be acceptable in both aspects and also things that aren't written down, valuing craft: textiles, fabrics, patterns, fibres, these specific techniques; these are histories, these are archives that need to be acknowledged and valued in the same way as like a cited paper by a white academic textile historian etc. It's like, why don't we actually talk to the Bangladeshi communities, about what their experiences are, rather than things that are just found in the V&A [the Victoria and Albert Museum].

Fadhel: [00:41:24] How are we for time? Do you have time for one more question?

Raisa: [00:41:30] Yes, we could do one more.

Fadhel: [00:41:32] This is sort of a two part question, but they go into each other... I want to end on language and expression.

Again, I was brought up in Sweden. Simply put, I identify as Swedish with a Tunisian background... Swedish is my first language and it is where I grew up. I don't speak Arabic. I see myself as part of the 'in-betweenship' of cultures. Friends in Sweden, whose parents are both immigrants, have a completely different lived experience than me, even if with its similarities... I have a gateway into Swedish culture that they don't. I can sort of empathise with both sides since I'm in the middle.

I'm wondering about the transition to a new place through immigration... Does that dilute or just simply evolve a culture naturally? In terms of embracing new ways of being, in the freedom to express queerness etc.?

Raisa: [00:42:24] I mean, my mum and dad came to the UK in the 60s, and then my sisters were born in the 70s, so they're almost like the bridge generation. I was born in the late 80s, coming up into the 90s. Even though I am, I don't know if it is first or second generation, I'm born of parents who weren't born here. So, I'm the first generation to be born here, both my sisters were too, but they lived through an entirely different generation. They had to suffer a lot of those kind of hard years during the 70s and 80s, where when you're an immigrant, you have to learn an entirely new culture: language, cultural beliefs, customs. You're navigating and learning so much, and yes, mistakes and like, horrible mix-ups happen. Then, with the horrible racism in the 70s and 80s, obviously, you know, it doesn't go away, but [today] it's not as violent as what my sisters went through. I think my mum was amazing. She did want to leave Bangladesh, because she's a feminist and she worked as a social worker. I think in another world she would be, she is, an artist.

In terms of the kind of language and dilution of culture, she tried to teach my sisters [Bangla], but then she also was like: *I'm not going to impose anything on you. Do whatever you want.* My mother was also told by school teachers to not speak Bangla at home, as that would impede our English. So, my mum stopped. So my sisters lost the full ability to speak, read and write Bengali. I would say that my sisters cleaved more into being British and English, my mum and dad just couldn't afford to take them back to Bangladesh early enough. They went when they were maybe like eleven, twelve, and that's a little bit late. I went to Bangladesh when I was two, three, and six. I have that grasp on the language, I can read and write, in a very basic way, but I can and I love that. I love that I can read phonetic transliteration and understand... That is a very beautiful thing. I wish I could learn so much more. I even considered taking classes, but the bittersweetness is that my sisters and me, we learned English very well and that did help our education. So with diaspora there is loss, there is grief... Our parents sacrificed so much, so we could have different opportunities.

But [at the same time] it's just a horrible trade-off. My mum didn't teach my sisters Bangla properly, because she was told by teachers: *Don't speak Bangla at home, don't teach them, otherwise they won't grasp better English.* That's such a grief, because obviously it is way more beautiful to be bilingual and have two languages. But, that is a kind of cultural hangover that's very apparent, it is a kind of racism where [they say]: *Don't teach them the other language, just English*. I am very lucky. I speak English very well, but it's very sad to have lost something like that.

Speaking from the diaspora, I don't know if it dilutes... People are forever going to be new migrants, new diasporas [will form], it is the way of the world. It's constantly happening; we're seeing climate disaster, there is going to be a lot of climate refugees, even though, politically, across the world, people don't want migrants, and certain places of the world are going to become completely uninhabitable and inhospitable. This is what will happen.

I know that, like, usually when people are [in the diasporas], it's the consequence of things like partition, living in lands of wars—a result of colonial, foreign policies. We need to look back at this hundreds and hundreds of years in time, not in just the recent fifty, we need to look back a lot further to understand what these questions/patterns are. Why is there such a massive community of Kashmiri people in the UK? Well, it's linked to British foreign policy, also linked to partition. We can see why there is a huge Turkish population in Germany. You see where these wars are, these faculties.

We have to understand why this is happening, and you asked about diluting and things like that... My work is very specifically from a diasporic perspective. I didn't grow up in Bangladesh, and when I go to Bangladesh, I know I can always leave. There are some people who are desperate to leave, they can't find security or home. It's very difficult to have a good standard of living, even if very basic, a comfortable living standard costs a lot of money... I think just like being a bridge and understanding that you have a specific viewpoint, you can see things from a specific, multiple, dual narrative perspective, which I think is an advantage. But also, that can bring up a lot. I don't know if that answers your question.

Fadhel: [00:48:10] That's great, I think we've sort of gone full circle now with everything we've touched upon.

My last question is about this cultural evolution that we just spoke about. You mentioned something about being a bridge... Does this cultural evolution, because in my experience it does, intersect with the representation and celebration of queer perspectives?

Raisa: [00:48:38] I mean, I think a lot of the South Asian people that I know in the UK, or in the US who came on student visas, who are queer, or trans-people, they came because it's much easier to live their lives fully, especially if you're trans. We wish we could be in Dhaka and be protected in the same way. Obviously it is very beautiful to be back home, but not to idolise either or... It's very difficult to answer this question because then it just perpetuates the idea of the West as more free. I don't want to play into that, because obviously we would love to just be in our homes, in the countries of our grandparents' birth and feel accepted.

What I will say is, a lot of these colonial laws, again, intersect with [religion], and we could say that everywhere, in Christian countries in Africa, where they have these colonial laws that were imposed and perpetuated through missionary education systems. I think it's just really important to be like, yes, we find freedom when we meet our communities in these diasporic, queer enclaves. But that doesn't mean they don't exist in Africa, in Asia, and in Bangladesh, these are very beautiful places as well.

103

When people have the [privilege to acquire] immigration [documents] and the VISAs [needed to migrate], people have found freedom in meeting with the kind of global communities in London, New York, or Paris. What I will say is that actually this perpetuation of *the West is better* is not true, because if you're in the middle of, like, Wyoming or something, or I don't know, somewhere like... Kent, or like, in the Isle of Wight, you would not find the freedom and the joy of the [queer] community. It has nothing really to do with the fact that countries are more free than not, it's just the fact that there is a queer diaspora, queer people have moved to cities and created communities, that's where you find the joy and the connection, and you will find this in every city, globally, even if they have punitive laws. The point is, those queer enclaves, hoping to fight for freedom, exist in all places around the world. The West is not the only free place to be whoever you are; [there is] a lot of violence, and a lot of discrimination.

Raisa Kabir is an interdisciplinary artist and weaver. Kabir uses woven text/textiles and performance to materialise multiple concepts, concerning the interwoven cultural politics of cloth. Kabir's work draws on textile mobilities, embodied archives, and geographies of anti-colonial resistance. Kabir's (un)weaving performances and tapestries use queer entanglement to complicate structures of power, global production/extraction, and to call on the weaving knowledge systems and technologies' potential, to transform, remagine and reweave the world structures we live under.

Kabir has exhibited work internationally at The Whitworth, Liverpool Biennial, Whitechapel Gallery, Australian Design Centre, Asia Art Now Paris, India Art Fair, Raven Row, The Craft Council London, CCA Glasgow, Archive Berlin, British Textile Biennial, Glasgow International, Textile Arts Center NYC, Ford Foundation Gallery NYC, and the Center for Craft, Creativity, and Design NC.

Kabir has lectured and shared her research at Tate Modern, the V&A, The Courtauld, and the Royal College of Art.

HERITAGE, HEDARED AND THE SEVEN DISTRICTS

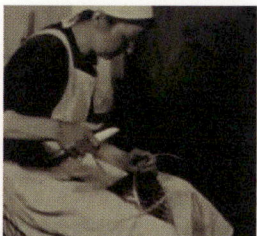

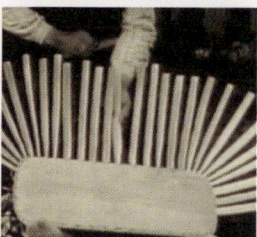

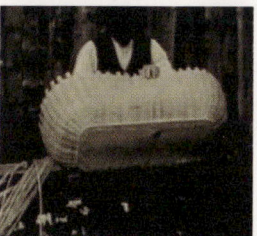

BEFORE BORÅS WAS FOUNDED, the lack of established cities within Sjuhärad, and the close proximity to foreign borders, created a widespread and lucrative black market.[1] As early as the 13th century, records show how the principle of limiting and prohibiting rural trade emerged. Merchants or farmers who were 'not townsfolk' were only to trade within a city, and 'solely within the town square'.[2] Later on, the continued prevalence of a black market, exacerbated by the fact that taxes were only collected within the borders of a city, led King Gustav II Adolf to forbid trading for farmers not residing within a town. As a result, the rural communities in Sjuhärad were forced to either cease trading or form a new town. Naturally, a majority chose the latter to protect their economic interests, hence the founding of Borås.[3] The city's charter declared that merchants residing within its borders were allowed to continue trading across the country, enjoying special customs-related privileges granted by the authority of the monarch.[4]

The economic importance of trading handcrafted objects for the rural communities, and the economic hardships which were instigated by the restriction of rural trading, led to a reversal of the edict just half a century later by the new monarch Karl XI.[5] His government accepted the need for farmers to trade goods without living within a city, and their rights were reinstated. In a letter to the local governor, King Karl XI stated that the farmers of Sjuhärad, due to their 'impoverished state' and ancient claim to handicraft, should 'unperturbed enjoy the freedom of trade that has happened since long gone ages'.[6]

***

In the paper 'The Hidden Economy' (1978), author Agneta Boqvist presents an ethnological study demonstrating the 'patterns of production and economic structure' in Bollebygd, a neighbouring district to Veden, between 1850 and 1950. Boqvist uses historical records to showcase the socioeconomic variables between specific groups of artisans who were active in the local cottage industry. One section describes that the reasons for the often site-specific nature of local practices are many and hard to pinpoint.[7] Boqvist notes that proximity to land allowed artisans to devote themselves to specific wooden handicrafts that suited their geographic location.

Access to woodland was a defining economic factor for local households, as it acted as a means to supplement the poor soil: offering pasture for cattle or raw materials to supply handicrafts.[8]

The economic investment needed to practice specific crafts greatly affected a household's choice of income source.[9] The paper mentions the makers of the *Ballebo* furniture, unique to the district of Bollebygd. Furniture making, a resource-heavy practice, demanded a 'considerable investment' of labour and material, and often had the 'character' of being the primary source of livelihood, making such a practice most common among households with the necessary resources readily available.[10]

In addition to having adequate resources (land, labour and material), having access to the right equipment and proper tools for production was another variable that influenced a household's choice in practising local crafts—furniture making often mandated a particular combination of tools, only used for the production of specific products.[11]

Basketry, on the other hand, required fewer and more modest means, mere domestic tools such as a knife and an axe. As such, in contrast to furniture making, it was a practice concentrated amongst the less fortunate with little resources available beyond the bare essentials.[12]

In one passage, Boqvist mentions Hedared as the local epicentre for basket making,[13] and argues that the public consensus on the average craftsperson as landless and impoverished, as being a maker was '...an occupation that did not bring its practitioners any greater social standing',[14] was a false 'freehand drawing' of reality.[15] The paper debates that although poor crofters originated other forms of local basketry (and depended on it as a means of economic survival during winters), its practice was soon embraced by small landowning farmers who began weaving baskets as an alternative stream of income.[16]

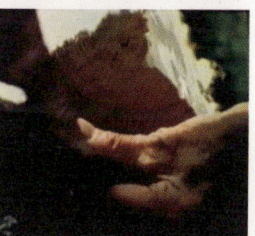

  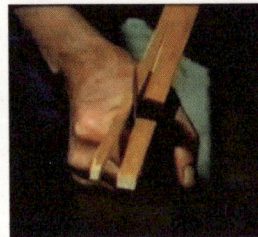

  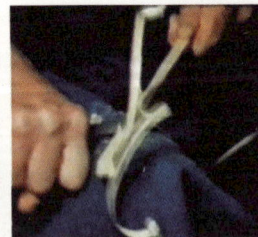

 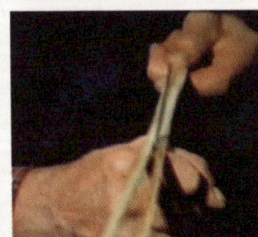 

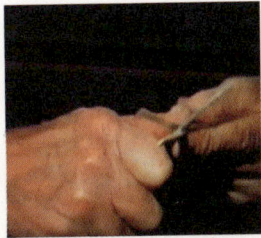
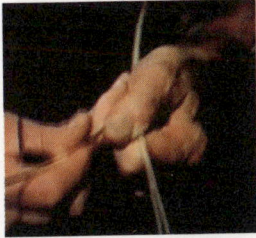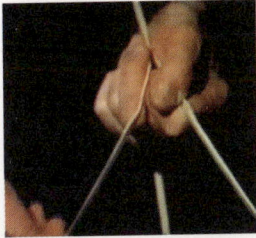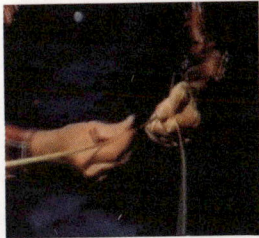
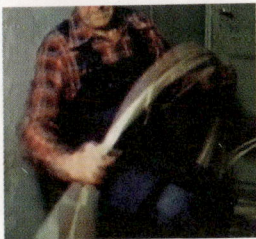
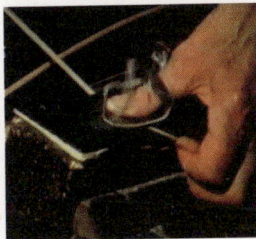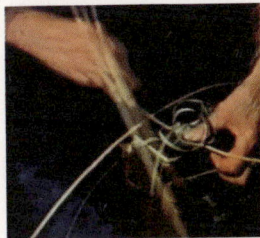
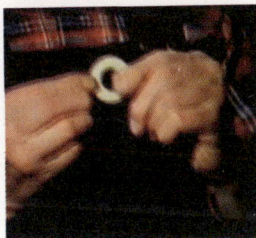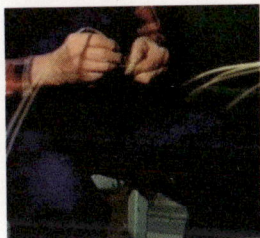

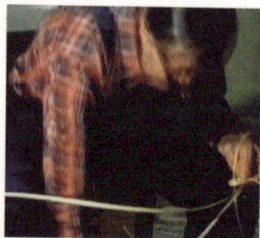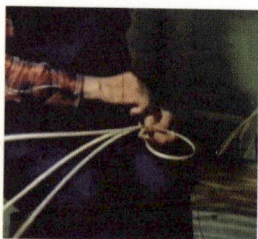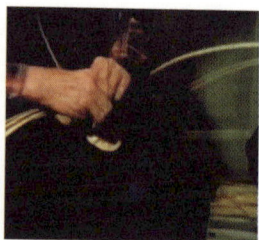

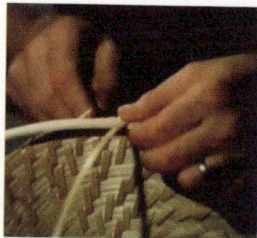

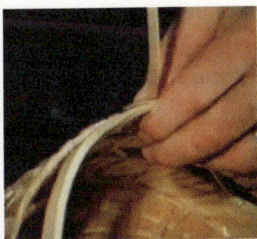  

  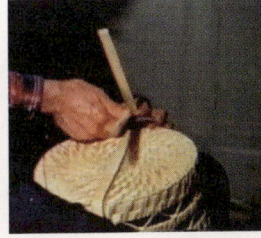
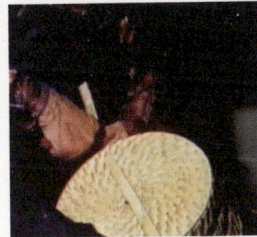  

115

Exemplified in Hedared, where the majority of its population: crofters, farmers and landowners alike were active makers.[17]

The social standing of local basket makers may have varied slightly. However, there was a clear distinction between practising households with steady access to necessary resources; those who became practitioners for additional income, and those that simply made do with what was around them: those who relied on basketry out of necessity, as a primary source of income. Whilst nuance may have existed locally, the legacy of the Hedared basket continues to highlight its past maker as belonging to the lower sections of society.

***

The granddaughter of 'the last basket maker', Ulla Petterson (b. 1965), recalls having had a great interest in basket making during her childhood. Growing up in Hedared, she was regularly exposed to traces of the basket in the nearby home of her grandfather. In one of our many conversations, Ulla spoke of how, when she approached Lennart and asked to participate, to learn the process of the craft, he dismissively refused.

As a child, Lennart's role was to assist in the family's daily operations, which used the handicraft as a means for survival. Only by necessity had he been introduced and (in some senses) made to participate in basket making. With time, Ulla came to understand that his emotional reaction stemmed from his upbringing. Her grandfather was the unintentional artisan.

One can only assume that Lennart's wishes for future generations of the Pettersson family were to be offered the luxury of choice—to not inherit his lack of social standing, the social stigma of having to make in order to survive, but instead be free to form their own sense of identity, led by possibility rather than necessity.

In the anthology series *Fässingen* (1996), Bengt K.Å. Johansson, former governor of the local county of Älvsborg (where Sjuhärad is located) writes:

In the district of Veden, there was never any rich soil, nothing has been given. The people had to work hard for their bread and stay inventive to make ends meet. Perhaps it is this that has coloured their mindset: shy of arrogance in favour of diligence and perseverance.[18]

The activities in the village of Hedared embody Johansson's words. The Hedared basket was born from its makers' long-standing familiarity with their local environment. It serves as a coherent example of how the inhabitants of Veden translated and combined their intimate knowledge of their surroundings with the determination and *need* to create a reliable income.

The complex methodology of the Hedared basket—both its material procurement and processing—was, and remains, primarily known only by Sjuhärad locals. The site-specific nature of its material process allowed for a language to form around the making; the act of crafting when making a basket was translated into the term *att korga* ('to basket') by locals.[19]

When working in Risa together with master basket maker Curt Bengtsson, I witnessed this local method first-hand, seeing how the annual rings from pine trees are extracted as a string-like material used to weave a basket. Although Bengtsson uses pine as his primary material, historically, both pine and fir were used. These trees were favoured for their local accessibility and high resin content, which made them easier to bend and shape during the making.

The Hedared basket's material process begins with finding the ideal *senvuxen* pine—a tree that has been growing for eighty to one hundred years, allowing its annual rings to form in unison. Suitable trees can be identified by a few simple visual cues: growing on a flat surface, having a small crown, and a stem that rises twig-free for at least two metres from the ground **1**. If sticks and branches have started to form on the stem, the wood cannot be processed for its annual rings. Once a possible candidate is found that fits this description, a section of its bark is knocked off **2** to expose the fibres

117

below **3**. These fibres, the 'surface wood' below the bark (that holds the annual rings), should grow in a straight, vertical direction to be processed successfully. Fibres leaning to the right are often useless, but fibres leaning (ever so slightly) to the left can be deemed good enough. Once a tree is taken down **4**, the log is split in two with the help of oak wedges **5**.

It is then split into quarters and the core wood is removed **6**, as it is not suitable for basket making. Once the logs have been split and cored **7**, they are kept in water for a minimum of three months **8**. During this time, a rotting process begins, making the bark slowly fall off by itself **9**.
When taken out of the water, it is then cut with great precision into narrow planks, with clearly visible annual rings stacked on top of each other **10**.

The procuring of the annual rings can then commence. Starting from the core and moving outwards, a slow knife is repeatedly chipped in between the annual rings **11**, dividing the plank into thinner sections **12**. This process is repeated until only single annual rings remain which can be split by hand **13**. Throughout the process, the wood is kept wet to make sure it is more malleable, and to minimise the risk of it splitting. The grip of the wooden plank is essential to maintain balance when separating the annual rings, string by string, and to ensure no unwanted splitting or cracking across them. The aim is to let the fibres naturally separate in a straight line, to 'evenly split' across their full length—what the locals call *rätklövet*. Once a plank is fully processed, the annual rings are drawn through an adjustable planer **14** to ensure uniformity in thickness and in colour. Only then is the material ready for basket weaving **15**.

The ability to process pine in this way requires a strong familiarity and understanding of the material's properties at each stage.

It becomes easy to understand why, historically, practising basket makers introduced their children to this labour-intensive process early on, knowing that the future economic welfare of the entire family would depend on it.

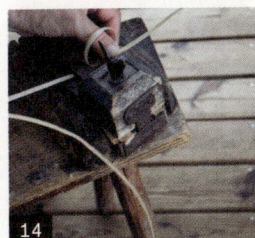
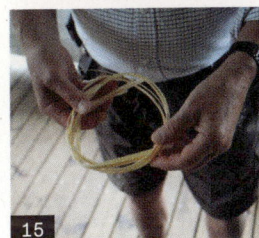

NOTES

1. Ljungström, C.J. (1865) *Åhs och Wedens härader samt staden Borås*, cited in Moritz, M. (1917) *Sveriges Officiella Statistik. Socialstatistik: Svensk Hemindustri—Del II*. Stockholm: Isaac Marcus' Boktryckeri–Aktiebolag, p. 10.
2. Moritz, M. (1917) 'Hemindustrin i södra Älvsborgs län—Historiska notiser: 1. Gårdfarihandel och hemindustri'. In: *Sveriges Officiella Statistik. Socialstatistik: Svensk Hemindustri—Del II*. Stockholm: Isaac Marcus' Boktryckeri–Aktiebolag, p. 10.
3. Ibid.
4. Ibid.
5. Ibid., p. 11.
6. Hufwedsson Dal, N. (1719) *Boërosia*, quoted in Moritz, M. (1917) *Sveriges Officiella Statistik. Socialstatistik: Svensk Hemindustri—Del II*. Stockholm: Isaac Marcus' Boktryckeri–Aktiebolag, p. 11. Translated by the author.
7. Boqvist, A. (1978) *Den Dolda Ekonomin—En etnologisk studie av Näringsstrukturen i Bollebygd 1850–1950*. Lund: LiberLäromedel/Gleerup, p. 26.
8. Ibid., p. 55.
9. Ibid., p. 138.
10. Ibid., pp. 137–138.
11. Ibid., p. 26.
12. Lithberg (1921), cited in Boqvist (1978), p. 58.
13. Boqvist (1978), p. 32.
14. Nylén (1968), cited in Boqvist (1978), p. 58. Translated by the author.
15. Boqvist (1978), p. 58.
16. Bäckström (1953), cited in Boqvist (1978), p. 58.
17. Boqvist (1978), p. 58.
18. Johansson, B.K.Å. (1996) 'Inledning'. In: Wiklund, N. (Ed.), *Fässingen—Från Borås och De Sju Häraderna: Tema Vedens Härad*. Borås: Kulturhistoriska Föreningen, p. 9. Translated by the author.
19. Östgård, K. (1996) 'Hedaredskorgar'. In: Wiklund, N. (Ed.), *Fässingen—Från Borås och De Sju Häraderna: Tema Vedens Härad*. Borås: Kulturhistoriska Föreningen, p. 61.

FURTHER READING

Andersson Palm, L. (2005) *Borås stads historia I: stad och omland fram till 1800-talets mitt*. Lund: Historiska Media.

Sterner, B. (1973) *Textil hemindustri i Sjuhäradsbygden under 1900-talets första hälft*. Stockholm: LT.

Widell, A. (2002) 'Gustav Persson—En studie av den siste korgmakaren i Hedared'. In: *Sjuhäradsbygdens kulturarv och historiska samhällsutveckling*. Borås: Högskolan i Borås.

IMAGE CREDITS

p. 107:
Lenk, T. (1923) *Korgmakeri: Upptagen i Hedared, Älvsborgs län*. Stockholm: SF.
pp. 110–115:
Film stills: Jansson, I. (1978) *Slöjd från Sjuhärad: Korgslöjd i Hedared*. Borås: De sju häradernas hemslöjdsförening/Slöjd i Väst/Kulturförvaltningen VGR.
p. 119:
Procuring annual rings in pine (2020/n.d.). Photo: Fadhel Mourali/Curt Bengtsson.

*OBJECT
ARCHIVED*

THE SOCIAL AND CULTURAL IMPORTANCE of the crafted objects originating from Sjuhärad is visible in the modern-day preservation of these traditional crafts in the local museums and their accompanying collections. I visited the archive at Borås Museum of History, with curator Catarina Ingemarsson to examine their collection of Hedared baskets.

As a space dedicated to preserving the region's collective memory, the museum's collections offer an overview of Sjuhärad's historical identity through the curation of items ranging from woven wooden baskets to mid-twentieth century plastic utility objects. Ingemarsson explained that the museum's vision is to assemble a group of objects whose individual stories offer clear and unique local insights, while also resonating with the region's broader historical narrative. She elaborated that an object's eligibility for the collection is determined by how well its story reflects Sjuhärad's histories at large.

In the case of the Hedared basket, its distinct narrative is found through its high level of craftsmanship, unique material process, and long heritage of site-specific making. The archived Hedared baskets are stored alongside other kinds of basketry from several parts of the Seven Districts, providing a comparative overview of the differences in aesthetics, material, technique, and historical function.

> ...the archive affirms the past, present, and future; it preserves the records of the past and it embodies the promise of the present to the future.[1]

Catarina described Hedared basket maker Gustav Persson (1923–2013) as very open and enthusiastic when given the opportunity to present his artisan skills to the public at the museum. Persson inherited the role of being 'the last basket maker' following the passing of Lennart Pettersson in the mid-1980s. Twenty years Lennart's junior, Gustav had a similar upbringing, as the child of makers who were part of the cottage industry in Hedared.

Gustav was the mentor of present-day Hedared basket maker Curt Bengtsson. Curt described a memory of working

122

with Persson: one day, before commencing his making, Gustav rolled down the curtains in his workshop, reluctant to let outsiders see him work. When Bengtsson asked why, he was met with a reaction similar to the one Ulla Pettersson received from Lennart when she expressed an interest in learning how to make baskets—a quick, dismissive reaction that shut down any further, or future, seemingly inapt, queries. The inherent sense of shame connected to the social origins of the Hedared basket is reflected in these stories, collected from its most prominent makers, both having lived the conditions determined by necessity and survival.

Ingemarsson described how modern-day artisans are generationally and socio-economically distant from the harsh realities that originated most local handicrafts. Crafting, no longer driven by necessity, has become a deliberate practice defined by the pursuit of knowledge, and mastering of rare skills. The act of crafting is, therefore, not only of cultural-historical importance but equally an act of tribute to the past owners of such knowledge.

The skill needed to produce the Hedared basket is now steeped in the muscle memory of Curt Bengtsson. He is the current 'last maker' (inheriting the title held by Gustav before him). The preservation of tradition through current-day artisans like Curt fosters a sense of recognition for them as the keepers of forgotten knowledge and for the origins of their specific craft.

In Curt's case, recognition of the modest means and scarce living conditions that made Hedared's unique basketry method. Bengtsson's practice is defined by the positive aspects of keeping the Hedared tradition alive; by contrast, he is the first of its acknowledged 'last makers' to be separated from its origins and the sense of internalised shame that defined its making by past practitioners.

As the continuation, and simultaneous making of heritage, Bengtsson's work encapsulates all of these elements, but most of all, his active practice helps to shape the public perception of the heritage—connected to the Hedared baskets in Borås museum's archive.

Memory, at once impoverished and enriched, presents itself as a device measurement, the 'ruler' of narrative.[2]

In the essay *On Longing* (1993) author Susan Stewart describes nostalgia as 'the desire for desire.'[3] Stewart argues that disconnections arise between our experience of time and our perception of reality when we engage with reproductions of the past. These disconnections, sustained through reproductions, are fed by constructed narratives that influence our perception of the present, and guide our outlook on the past it depicts:

> By the narrative process of nostalgic reconstruction the present is denied and the past takes on an authenticity of being, an authenticity which, ironically, it can achieve only through narrative.[4]

A film documenting the material process of the Hedared basket conveying its 'true essence', and recreating the feeling of being there in person, is built on a constructed narrative. In the guise of reconstruction, the disconnection between the reality of the past experience and one's present perception of it, generates a longing, a craving for the experience itself, which is what Stewart describes as nostalgia—'the desire for desire.'

> Nostalgia, like any form of narrative, is always ideological: the past it seeks has never existed except as narrative, and hence, always absent, that past continually threatens to reproduce itself as felt lack.[5]

This craving fuels nostalgia as a response: a steered, narrated longing to something perceived as simpler, purer, and more authentic. In the context of the basket: a return to an authenticated, unmediated, trusted, and 'true way' of practice, as presented in the documentary featuring Lennart or in the short film *Gustav Persson: Basket Maker in Hedared* (2004).

The duty of the craft, to convey its sense of authenticity and 'true essence', becomes evident when its past makers gained institutional and cultural recognition as a practitioner bearing knowledge of cultural-historical importance.

This sense of duty overrode any feelings of personal discomfort (stemming from a previous lack of social prominence). Seemingly, practising a craft like the one found in the Hedared basket bestows a sense of belonging to the practitioner, as they become part of a long lineage of site-specific makers and a member of a small group of acknowledged practitioners.

When I asked Ingemarsson, why a handicraft practice would historically be a source of great shame to its maker, she reacted with surprise. After all, the Hedared basket as a practice had been nothing but publicly celebrated, most notably through repeated documentation throughout the twentieth century, as seen in the documentary featuring Lennart or in the short film with Gustav. These films were made to preserve the memory of the craft and its knowledge—a celebratory act recognising its past local impact and continued significance.

Looking at the footage from these films today, they are imbued with a revered 'vintage feel' and nostalgic ambience, one that reinforces the notion of the basket as something of a historical enigma. The narrative of both films positions the Hedared basket as something not of the present, but of the past, where the practice of its 'last maker' continuously saves it from extinction. Such a narrative, infused with a nostalgic tint, also reiterates the notion of loss—a loss of something that is found through these rare artisans, who single-handedly keep its tradition (and pieces of our collective memory) alive through their practice.

The iteration of artisans as gatekeepers, stemming from such documentation, also sets the tone for how artefacts such as the basket are remembered and experienced in spaces like the museum. It creates the default for how the basket, and by extension, the wider notion of our collective cultural heritage, is publicly regarded. By reproductions, the archived Hedared baskets remain mere symbols of pride for regional traditions, sources of an agrarian and diligent past. From such symbolism, the basket is trapped under a historical veil, distancing it from the present. It is never to be fully understood. Instead, it is simply a thing to be remembered or a practice to be admired. Without understanding the present-day necessity of the archival objects, but only their historical, *nostalgic* narratives, the Hedared baskets in the museum's collection are left mere symbols, anonymous vessels that bear witness to the Sjuhärad region as a place with deep craft-related roots. This lays further emphasis on current-day makers as saviours, keepers of such remembrance, which in turn exacerbates the notion of loss, allowing the cycle of its 'last maker' to continue in perpetuity.

> Nostalgia is the repetition that mourns the inauthenticity of all repetition and denies the repetition's capacity to form identity.[6]

It is easy to recognise the basket for its impactful historical narrative. Yet, there is a danger when brought into the archival space, that the present-day necessity of an object such as the Hedared basket is somewhat overlooked. When it is only experienced by the public through various acts of preservation, the favour of historical reverence hinders it from coming alive under new circumstances. If the Hedared basket is to be more than a historical heritage, i.e. something belonging to the past, the ways in which its legacy is presented to the public by historic institutions is key. For it to be experienced as a living, breathing entity, the Hedared basket must be given room to exist beyond the confines of nostalgia. To find new contexts, its survival cannot (and should not) continuously be presented as precarious—in a permanent state of limbo.

Today, the basket's role as a cultural-historical artefact is to remain as such—preserved as an object to be revered within the archive, or admired through the continuation of its practice by a 'last maker'.

***

In the 1957 essay collection *Mythologies*, French philosopher Roland Barthes describes plastic as 'the stuff of alchemy', as a 'miraculous substance' that transforms from raw matter to 'the finished, human object'—'two extremes' with nothing between them 'but a transit, hardly watched over by an attendant in a cloth cap, half-god, half-robot'.[7]

Plastic, 'the very idea of infinite transformation',[8] then new to the market, was (and, of course, still is) made to be used. It remains a material cheap to produce (and transform) into an abundant supply chain of readily available goods. Found in every household, 'it is ubiquity made visible'.[9] Plastic's 'prosaic character' was seen by Barthes as its 'triumphant reason' for existing, 'for the first time, artifice aims at something common, not rare'.[10]

In the same archival space as the publicly revered Hedared basket—an artefact embodying site-specific ingenuity, generational knowledge, and skill that transcends any recollection of the actual period from which it originated (the actual age of the Hedared basket is that of myth, deeply rooted in the village soil), there were objects made out of plastic.

I found myself startled.

Ingemarsson quickly replied to my query as to why this was the case, with a simple answer: it is simply in line with the museum's archival mission. Following Borås Museum of History's fundamental policy for its collection—to obtain items with a distinct narrative in close connection to regional history—their acquisition of plastic objects began after plastic entered the mainstream during the 1960s. Ingemarsson spoke of plastic as initially seen as a great innovation, a democratic medium that meant more people had access to more affordable everyday items and newer 'things'.

> Plastic is wholly swallowed up in the fact of being
> used: ultimately, objects will be invented for the
> sole pleasure of using them.[11]

Catarina explained that because Hedared baskets are made from pine, a commonly used and well-documented material, they are certain to continue standing fully intact in the archive for another 'four hundred years'. On the contrary, their neighbouring artefacts made out of plastic, may not even survive the century. Despite the permanence of microplastics, a plastic object's ability to remain *intact* for as long as its archived, pine-built counterpart, remains to be seen.

Ingemarsson added that these elusive properties are a great cause of concern for museum curators. The uncertainty surrounding the ability of plastic objects to remain intact stems from the fact that plastic is a relatively young material. Its long-term durability and behaviours are not fully understood, as it has only been widely used for a few decades.

Therefore, understanding the variables of its ageing processes and knowing the appropriate preservation methods to apply, is limited and largely uncharted. The material continues to stand in stark contrast to the organic properties of the pine used in the baskets, which must grow for nearly a century before it *possibly* qualifies to become its raw material.

> The hierarchy of substances is abolished: a single one replaces them all: the whole world can be plasticized...even life itself...[12]

Still, in the repository space used to store its collection, the traces of the man-made and industrial in the plastic artefacts become regarded as equally precious to the pine that makes up the handcrafted baskets. When a new object is accepted into Borås Museum's collection, it, and by default its material, gains recognition for its unique narrative and impactful contribution to regional history—*worthy* of being preserved, and having its story narrated as part of the region's collective storytelling. Meaning that plastic, this cheap, mundane and readily accessible material, holds the same value as the precious, ingenious pine that makes up the Hedared basket. Within the archive, both become significant markers in the timeline of Sjuhärad's regional history.

***

While the role of plastic holds value in itself (as a metaphor for contemporary material culture within Borås Museum's archive), the questionable longevity of the plastic object suggests a lingering uncertainty that is comparable to the future legacy of making in the Seven Districts.

When I asked Ingemarsson what she thought of as the future legacy of making in the region, she was unsure. The disappearance of the cottage industry in Sjuhärad was brought on by the development of Borås as an urban area with its emerging industry. In the early twentieth century, a booming textile industry prompted a shift in making, from domestic crafting to industrial production. The emergence of the textile industry in the Seven Districts resulted in a societal shift, as the subsistence of necessity fuelling the cottage industry became a thing of the past. New, reliable streams of income were readily available through factory employment. It offered an alternative to tedious and labour-intensive crafting, often attracting a younger generation of rural workers to move to Borås.

In the lecture, 'Borås and the Urban Breakthroughs',[13] Johannes Daun, historian at the Textile Museum of Sweden (the sister museum of Borås Museum of History) filters Swedish urbanisation history through a Borås-centred lens. Daun divides the term 'urbanisation' into three categories:

Demographic Urbanisation: Cities have a denser population than rural areas as people move from the countryside to urban centres. For example, the textile industry in Borås helped to further populate the city.

Structural Urbanisation: Cities develop essential infrastructure and services, such as railways, roads, and communication networks.

Cultural Urbanisation: Urban centres influence societal norms, customs, and practices, spreading from the city to broader society.

The urbanisation of Borås marked the beginning of a cultural shift, a new era defined by accessibility and possibility. Access to the infrastructural comforts of a city gave rural labourers, such as Lennart, the possibility to leave behind a previous lack of social prominence when working within the new industries forming in the city.

Susan Stewart (1993) describes the discourse of the city as 'syncretic', one that is 'political in its untranslatability',[14] quoting Austrian philosopher Ludwig Wittgenstein:

> Our language can be seen as an ancient city:
> a maze of little streets and squares, of old and
> new houses with additions from various
> periods; and this surrounded by a multitude of
> new boroughs with straight regular streets and
> uniform houses.[15]

Historically, the local tradesmen, knallarna, developed their own sayings and took on loan words from other languages, gathered under the umbrella of Månsing. Rural artisans in Hedared developed unique expressions in relation to describing the Hedared basket's making process. Later, in places like Hulta, the regional version of Västgötska met a new variant of Swedish, Förortssvenska.

Such local evolutions become more evident in the city as a centralised urban hub, where the continuous development of the Swedish language finds new fuel by different cultures (quite literally) crossing paths, colliding, and/or coexisting. The ever-evolving structures of a city are a record that holds traces of its own linguistic histories. Locally, this is made tangible through Borås' own mazes of 'little streets and squares' and its various 'old and new houses with additions from various periods'.

Borås' pebble-stoned paths hold the scope of local semantics embedded in its very pavement—seen in the case of the historical Månsing scattered across the 'regular streets and uniform houses' of Hulta.

Borås is now no longer a primary place of production, but instead home to the headquarters of several textile and fast fashion corporations. The questionable longevity and temporary qualities of the plastic objects found in the archive, also draw parallels to these major fast fashion corporations—through their unsustainable practices: trading from standardised and globalised production chains that often disregard environmental or socioeconomic issues.

It is generally known that the Sjuhärad region is the place for textiles in Sweden. Ingemarsson explained that the current identity of the region is often defined by the previous large-scale textile industry, exemplified by the multiple headquarters with integrated design departments still based in the region. She reiterated the importance of an established connection between an object's own narrative and the region's broader histories for it to become part of their collection. Catarina highlighted that, generally speaking, there are contenders, yet none currently stand out as unique, with enough symbolism to connect them to regional history.

Ingemarsson continued to emphasise that it is from within the remnants of the previous industry (the companies still operating in the area) that future archival objects will eventually emerge. Despite her difficulty in identifying a contemporary candidate, a clear contender to become a future archival object, Catarina noted that the design element in current local practices generally acts as a common, immaterial beacon for the making still taking place in the region.

***

Pre-industry, knowing one's material was essential as a maker. It was a given when certain areas in Sjuhärad practised their own site-specific crafts. Hyper-localised hubs of knowledge (i.e. Hedared and its basketry) acted as the basis for the region's famed cottage industry. Borås' industry and the migration of rural workers into the city, posed a loss for both the need for ingenuity (the kind that made the basket) and the tangible handicraft skills connected to it.

The eventual loss of tangible skill, through the separation between maker and material, is evident in today's general lack of regional ownership over production processes (due to globalised production chains). During the cottage industry, the various tasks that built the Hedared basket were delegated and divided across entire families: the men of the family often procured its material, while women and children wove the actual object.

The industrial approach to making similarly delegated tasks, dividing the making process into distinct sections (i.e. a production line). Each section had its own profession attached to it. With time, rather than keeping the various stages of making concentrated in one place, the production in the Seven Districts would evolve to be locally designed but globally produced.

The shift in regional making went from prefacing, and relying on, localised knowledge in the cottage industry, to embracing a more generalised understanding of mass production: a mode of practice better suited for the industrial apparatus.

Simply put, one could argue that the traditional crafter, when placed within the city's industry, would either evolve into an 'industrial maker' part of a production line—acquiring the making skills needed to fulfil their section in the line of production—or develop into a more expressive role, adjacent to the actual making. The traditional crafter would then become the guiding element that deciphered how the product, garment or textile, took its form—i.e. a designer. In tandem with language fusing and new spoken iterations emerging and cementing themselves in Borås city, the entire device of industry marked the beginning of a new era.

The designer's skill set developed beyond the making of utilitarian objects to be traded. The access brought forward in this new era of possibility allowed the designer to engage with the language of a city. Its various iterations helped pinpoint target groups and guide the production of goods with aesthetic relevance or monetary value for a specific audience.

In other words, when deciphering the language of the city—'political in its untranslatability'—the designer used its 'syncretic discourse' to navigate the marketplace and create products that met its needs. This language (of consumption) did not condition the designer to relate to making through tradition, nor was its approach a given source of high craftsmanship—its purpose was to imagine and create possibility: goods that emphasised a new era in which necessity was inferior to possibility.

While most production lines have emigrated out of Sjuhärad, the design element remains firmly intact in the region. It continues to facilitate the language of the city and oversee global production chains. This not only reflects the former emergence of industrial production processes, but exemplifies the perceived immateriality of the current state of local making practices.

The designer, and the lasting design practices, continue to serve as a measure of the previous evolution, and the future legacy of making in the Seven Districts.

MATERIAL: FIR/PINE
TYPE: TRUNK
YEAR: EARLY 1900s
DIMENSIONS: 880 × 380 × 270
MAKER: UNKNOWN

MATERIAL: FIR/PINE
TYPE: FÖRNINGS BASKET
YEAR: 1970s
DIMENSIONS: 430 × 420 × 350
MAKER: LENNART PETTERSSON

MATERIAL: FIR/PINE
TYPE: FÖRNINGS BASKET
YEAR: 1970s
DIMENSIONS: UNKNOWN
MAKER: LENNART PETTERSSON

MATERIAL: FIR/PINE
TYPE: TRAY
YEAR: 1970s
DIMENSIONS: 420 × 430 × 60
MAKER: LENNART PETTERSSON

MATERIAL: PINE
TYPE: CHEESE BASKET
YEAR: 1990s
DIMENSIONS: 220 × 220 × 100
MAKER: GUSTAV PERSSON

MATERIAL: FIR/PINE
TYPE: CHEESE BASKET
YEAR: EARLY 1900s
DIMENSIONS: 490 × 490 × 140
MAKER: UNKNOWN

MATERIAL: PINE
TYPE: TRAYS
YEAR: 1970s
DIMENSIONS: VARIOUS
MAKER: LENNART PETTERSSON

MATERIAL: PINE
TYPE: SEWING BOX
YEAR: 1994
DIMENSIONS: 140 × 140 × 65
MAKER: GUSTAV PERSSON

MATERIAL: PINE
TYPE: KNÄCKEBRÖDS BASKET
YEAR: 1990s
DIMENSIONS: UNKNOWN
MAKER: GUSTAV PERSSON

MATERIAL: PINE
TYPE: KNÄCKEBRÖDS BASKET
YEAR: 2000s
DIMENSIONS: UNKNOWN
MAKER: GUSTAV PERSSON

MATERIAL: PINE
TYPE: TRAY
YEAR: 1990s
DIMENSIONS: 295 × 220 × 45
MAKER: GUSTAV PERSSON

MATERIAL: PINE
TYPE: TRAY
YEAR: 1990s
DIMENSIONS: 355 × 280 × 45
MAKER: GUSTAV PERSSON

MATERIAL: PINE/FIR
TYPE: MANGLE BASKET
YEAR: EARLY 1900s
DIMENSIONS: 920 × 550 × 290
MAKER: UNKNOWN

MATERIAL: PINE
TYPE: MANGLE BASKET
YEAR: 2011
DIMENSIONS: 590 × 360 × 170
MAKER: GUSTAV PERSSON

MATERIAL: PINE
TYPE: BERRY-PICKING BASKETS
YEAR: 1990s
DIMENSIONS: VARIOUS
MAKER: GUSTAV PERSSON, ULLA PETTERSSON

MATERIAL: PINE
TYPE: BERRY-PICKING BASKET
YEAR: EARLY TO MID-1990s
DIMENSIONS: 520 × 320 × 350
MAKER: UNKNOWN

MATERIAL: PINE/FIR
TYPE: COLOURED BERRY-PICKING BASKET
YEAR: 1920—30s
DIMENSIONS: 590 × 390 × 400
MAKER: UNKNOWN

MATERIAL: PINE/FIR
TYPE: COLOURED LOG BASKET
YEAR: UNKNOWN
DIMENSIONS: UNKNOWN
MAKER: UNKNOWN

MATERIAL: PINE/FIR
TYPE: LOG BASKET
YEAR: UNKNOWN
DIMENSIONS: UNKNOWN
MAKER: UNKNOWN

MATERIAL: PINE/FIR
TYPE: BOTTLE BASKETS
YEAR: UNKNOWN
DIMENSIONS: VARIOUS
MAKER: UNKNOWN

MATERIAL: PINE/FIR
TYPE: BOTTLE BASKET
YEAR: UNKNOWN
DIMENSIONS: UNKNOWN
MAKER: LENNART PETTERSSON

MATERIAL: PINE/FIR
TYPE: BOTTLE BASKET
YEAR: UNKNOWN
DIMENSIONS: UNKNOWN
MAKER: LENNART PETTERSSON

MATERIAL: PINE
TYPE: MINIATURE BASKET
YEAR: UNKNOWN
DIMENSIONS: 180 × 100 × 320
MAKER: UNKNOWN

MATERIAL: PINE
TYPE: TRAY
YEAR: UNKNOWN
DIMENSIONS: 250 × 250 × 220
MAKER: GUSTAV PERSSON

MATERIAL: PINE/FIR
TYPE: LAMP SHADE
YEAR: UNKNOWN
DIMENSIONS: UNKNOWN
MAKER: LENNART PETTERSSON

MATERIAL: PINE
TYPE: SHELF
YEAR: UNKNOWN
DIMENSIONS: 360 × 130 × 460
MAKER: UNKNOWN

MATERIAL: PINE
TYPE: KNITTING BASKET
YEAR: 2009
DIMENSIONS: UNKNOWN
MAKER: GUSTAV PERSSON

MATERIAL: PINE
TYPE: LAUNDRY BASKET
YEAR: 2010
DIMENSIONS: UNKNOWN
MAKER: GUSTAV PERSSON

NOTES

1. Manoff, M. (2004) 'Theories of the Archive from Across the Disciplines'. In: *Libraries and the Academy*, Volume 4—Number 1. Baltimore: The Johns Hopkins University Press, p. 11.
2. Stewart, S. (1993) 'On description and the book'. In: *On Longing: Narratives of the Miniature, the Gigantic, the Souvenir, the Collection*. Durham and London: Duke University Press, p. 24.
3. 'Hostile to history and its invisible origins, and yet longing for an impossibly pure context of lived experience at a place of origin, nostalgia wears a distinctly utopian face, a face that turns toward a future-past, a past which has only ideological reality. This point of desire which the nostalgic seeks is in fact the absence that is the very generating mechanism of desire [...] the re-alization of re-union imagined by the nostalgic is a narrative utopia that works only by virtue of its partiality, its lack of fixity and closure: nostalgia is the desire for desire.', Stewart, S. (1993) 'On description and the book'. In: *On Longing: Narratives of the Miniature, the Gigantic, the Souvenir, the Collection*. Durham and London: Duke University Press, p. 23.
4. Ibid., p. 23.
5. Ibid.
6. Ibid.
7. Barthes, R. (1972) 'Plastic'. In: *Mythologies*. Translated by Annette Lavers. New York: The Noonday Press, Farrar, Straus & Giroux, p. 97.
8. Ibid.
9. Ibid.
10. Ibid., p. 98.
11. Ibid., p. 99.
12. 'The hierarchy of substances is abolished: a single one replaces them all: the whole world *can* be plasticized, and even life itself since, we are told, they are beginning to make plastic aortas.', Barthes, R. (1972) 'Plastic'. In: *Mythologies*. Translated by Annette Lavers. New York: The Noonday Press, Farrar, Straus & Giroux, p. 99.
13. Daun, J. (2021) *Borås och det urbana genombrottet*. Online lecture. https://www.d7kf.se/2021/04/18/18-4-boras-och-det-urbana-genombrottet/ [29/01/24]. Translated by the author.
14. Stewart, S. (1993) 'Prologue'. In: *On Longing: Narratives of the Miniature, the Gigantic, the Souvenir, the Collection*. Durham and London: Duke University Press, p. 2.
15. Wittgenstein, L. (1958) *Philosophical Investigations*, quoted in Stewart, S. (1993), p. 1.

FURTHER READING

Assmann, J. and Czaplicka, J. (1995) 'Collective Memory and Cultural Identity'. In: *New German Critique*, Number 65, Cultural History/Cultural Studies, Spring–Summer, pp. 125–133.

Boym, S. (2001) *The Future of Nostalgia*. New York: Perseus Books Group.

Derrida, J. (1996) *Archive Fever: A Freudian Impression*. Chicago: The University of Chicago Press.

Leyson, B.W. (1944) *Plastics in the world of tomorrow*. New York: E.P. Dutton & Company Inc.

Meikle, J.L. (1995) *American Plastic: A Cultural History*. New Brunswick: Rutgers University Press.

Nord, A.G. and Tronner, K. (2012) *Plast: morgondagens kulturobjekt, projekt för bevarande av plastföremål—terminologi, analys, skador, nedbrytning, förvaring*. Stockholm: Riksantikvarieämbetet.

Tesar, M. (2012) 'Ethics and truth in archival research'. In: *Journal of the History of Education Society*, Volume 44, 2015—Issue 1, pp. 101–114.

IMAGE CREDITS

pp. 134–147:
Hedared baskets from the Pettersson family collection (2020). All images taken by the author.

FROM THE HEART
OF THE VILLAGE

MY EXPLORATION OF THE BASKET led me to explore the concept of belonging, which led me to delve into the depths of the
cultural and social conditions from which it had emerged.
The basket was, and still is, surrounded with a way of life that
is secondary to me. My perception of Västgötska, Hedared and
its rural way of life, stands as the epitome of what it means to
belong.

The initial stages of the research had pieced together
the elements that had shaped the basket and its heritage.
I had immersed myself in various sources: poring over books,
publications, records, and even visiting archives and recrea-
tions of historical housing. Each encounter with historical data
was enriched by personal anecdotes from family members,
who provided nuance into the Hedared basket's factual history
and the social conditions, the culture, that had birthed it.

Their insights led me to continue sourcing knowledge
beyond written, documented facts, and instead collect it directly from experts within their particular field—most notably from basket maker Curt Bengtsson. As a result, I have developed a long-standing friendship with Curt. Observing the
basket's material process, listening to Curt's stories, whilst
handling the core component of the basket—its material—
myself, made family anecdotes, and the histories encountered
through books, come to life in a tangible way.

The different ways of collecting the various aspects
to the basket's story, each provided a unique perspective on
its heritage, and each gave a new piece to the making of its
patchwork. Together, they revealed the inherent subjectivity
of historical narration. I had encountered the greater historical narrative of the village and its region, and if I had learnt
anything during this process of understanding, it was that
there is a depth to knowing that transcends mere written,
documented facts.

In my continued research, I sought to further comprehend the way of life in which the basket exists, and how
it differs from my own lived experience. I am connected to
Lennart by family and through the greater evolution of making
in Sjuhärad. We stand at opposite ends of its history. I wanted

to connect my personal narrative with the village's greater making-related narratives—what traces of the basket remain in its rural birthplace? How do its past cultural cues reveal themselves within the community today?

Continuing this exploratory venture went beyond merely poring over books, or gathering further anecdotes about past Hedared makers. Although delving deeper into the historical significance of the basket itself (through its past makers or otherwise) would be an essential part of mapping the present, my main objective was to continue using the basket as a conduit. Take its making-related narratives to continue detangling the web of intricacies between Lennart and me, my culture and his—find that sought-after mutual core.

The continued exploration necessitated clarity of purpose: it is the *heartfelt* that brings nuance to things. It is the vulnerability of the lived experience that helps to transcend beyond factual reasoning, allowing for the possibility of creating common ground between two distinct cultural spaces. I wanted to use this notion as a central element when making the basket's patchwork. The research, therefore, needed to encompass the broader community of Hedared.

I needed to listen to voices that were yet unfamiliar, take in new perspectives of the heritage, and process it through those who expressed themselves equally invested in the basket as I am. To lead a continued exploration with the heartfelt.

How do the present-day realities of the village differ from my own culture?

How do these realities reflect the idea of belonging?

Enter the second phase of the research:

In Thoughts, *Together*.

In 1954, the villagers of Hedared convened a meeting with the intention of establishing an organisation entrusted with the management of the old parish cottage and its surrounding plot of land. The Hedared Village Association was founded in 1956 when the community inherited the estate of Frans Berglund, the last resident of the cottage. Tasked with stewarding Berglund's assets, the association, composed of dedicated volunteers, has ever since been committed to preserving the community's history whilst working for its future development.

The association serves as Hedared's voluntary and democratic voice, advocating for community cohesion and fostering a shared sense of unity and progress in the village. All residents in the village are by default association members, with a fluctuating number of people actively participating in decision-making alongside the board—a chairman, deputy chairman, treasurer, etc.—who devote their time, expertise, and efforts to the interests of the village. It was through a series of conversations with members of the association that I was able to further unveil Hedared's past roots, present-day realities, and future legacies.

Together, we explored craftsmanship, social progression, and personal destinies—all interconnected via the heritage of the basket.

The texts, documents, photographs, and transcripts on the following pages comprise a simple collection of conversations, interactions and observations gathered during this specific research period. When working with the members of the association, I acquired a greater understanding of the basket as a community-bearing object, through the personal narrative of each participant.

The aim was to allow each conversation to steer the course of the research, starting with a common set of questions, and then letting the conversation evolve organically, enabling participants to share what they deemed relevant. This made any recurring themes to naturally change direction with each participant, and introduce new perspectives, locales, and historical individuals connected to the village.

What does the collective remembrance of a local craft heritage look like? Do memories differ from family to family? Person to person? How does such a heritage inform the current self-image of a rural area?

Through this trust-led exchange, I aimed to act as an interpreter: observing and synthesising the conversations. I visually translated each individual's narrative into imagery, linked it to village artefacts, or integrated it into my woven work.*

Reflecting on my original aspirations—understanding the cultural-historical significance, social influence, and contemporary relevance of the basket—working with the Village Association brought these concepts to life. Similarly to when handling the basket's raw material with basket maker Curt Bengtsson, these interactions rendered my prior anecdotes of the heritage into something tangible.

It opened up new avenues for understanding the structures that sustain this rural legacy today—how its remnants are remembered and governed. It led me closer to Lennart and his reality, to the greater parallels between his world and mine. Ultimately adding new pieces to the patchwork, and the much sought-after 'big picture'.

At the core of this endeavour lies the heart. I only seek for the generosity and openness of each participant to be met with sincerity and authenticity in this publication—for the up-coming section to be a projection of our moments of connection whilst being In Thoughts, *Together*.

Participating members:
Ulla Pettersson
Kent Schoultz
Jan Andersson
Lena Gustavsson
Ingemar Samuelsson

*This body of research serves as a series of testaments, relating to the larger themes of this book. Beyond this publication, the research would serve as the subject for my woven work—presented in the exhibition In Thoughts, *Together* hosted by Hemslöjden i Skåne in 2023. My ambition had been to focus on the collective. I was weaving with Lennart through my material, in dialogue with what remains of his legacy in the village.

THE SMELL IS MY FIRST MEMORY OF THE BASKET

In the olden days, it was quite common to include someone's occupation on their gravestone, at least if it was something to be proud of. At the cemetery in Hedared, you'll find Homestead Owners, Manufacturers, Bricklayers, and even a Former Soldier. One small, reclining gravestone right by the old entrance reads:

> BASKET MAKER
> AUGUST PEHRSSON
> 1845—1895
> HIS WIFE
> JOSEFINA
> 1850—1900
> LARSAGÅRDEN

Basket makers and basket weavers were commonplace in most households in Hedared back in the day, but as far as I know, this is the only one who proudly displayed it on their gravestone.

The smell of grandad's basket room is my earliest memory of the craft. The room wasn't a workshop, it was just a room. When he was making baskets, it was a basket room, when his brother-in-law visited, it was a bedroom. There are photographs inside of homes in Hedared from back then, showing villagers crafting inside their houses.

157

The craft was done at home with modest means, a knife, an awl, and a planer. Makers sat and worked in the kitchen in the evenings, or when they had no other chores. Not necessarily because they liked it, but to survive.

I call the scent of the material a smell because it's neutral. It can smell good or it can smell bad. If you've never smelt it, it's hard to describe. It's not at all cosy and woody like in a wood workshop. It's strong, sour, and pungent. It sticks to your hands and clothes. You sometimes need to wash your hands

once or even twice before it fades. But for me, this smell is grandad, childhood and the feeling of safety and comfort.

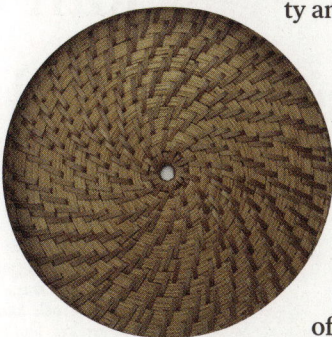

My mum worked as a care worker for the elderly, and one of the people she helped was grandad. He may have been able to go into the forest and fell trees, scythe a field, plant and harvest potatoes, cook pig feed, and tend to the pigs, but, according to the gender norms of the time, as a man, he wasn't trusted to clean and cook for himself.

So, while mum cleaned and cooked, I sat in the basket room and watched grandad work. When I got a bit older, I started to go to his house by myself. He would let me use his leftover material, and on one occasion I made an entire trivet. In my recollection, I, of course, made it all by myself. He had a small notebook where he wrote down orders for various baskets. Serving trays and förnings baskets were the most popular.

Sometimes we went to a stream a few hundred metres from his house to get new material. The wood had to be kept wet until it was processed to the right dimensions. That stream is now just a memory because the new landowner, me, hasn't properly maintained and dredged it.

159

Siste i Risa som kan fläta korg

I Hedared, där vägen Risa slutar, ligger Len Petterssons stuga. Han pensionär och kan ägna hur mycket han vill åt korgmakeri. Jordbruket tade han med vid pensi ringen. Förut blev arbet garna både fjorton och f ton timmar. Nu nöjer sig med att arbeta tre — ra timmar om dagen korgarna.

— Det är ett tidsförd säger han själv. Med "tidsfördriv" håller han tradition vid liv som in yngre har tid eller tålan att ta över. Han är den s korgmakaren i byn där en gång fanns 25 stycken.

— Se sidan 3 —

Lennart Pettersson med moralkniv som är det främ verktyget när en korg s blå till. Med sitt tidsförd håller han en gammal tr tion vid liv.

ÄN KAN HAN
—RISAS SISTE
KORGFLÄTARE

I seklets första decennier fanns det bortåt 25 korgmakare i Risa. Nu finns det bara en kvar. Lennart Pettersson heter han. och han har flätat korgar sedan han var sex år. Nu är han pensionär, men flätar fortfarande sina korgar.

Man tar av till vänster på den lilla grusvägen i Hedared. Risa står det på skylten. Vägen slingrar sig mellan fält och stugor. Den blir smalare. Det växer gräs mellan hjulspåren. Den skärps vid en liten gul stuga. Där, i Risa, bor korgmakare Lennart Pettersson.

— Förut när det var jordbruk på gården kunde man vara igång femton timmar om dagen, säger han. Men nu håller jag på med korgarna tre, fyra timmar. Det är ju ett tidsfördriv om inte annat.

Tradition

Men det är inte bara för att få tiden att gå som Lennart Pettersson flätar korgar. Han håller en gammal tradition vid liv.

— När det var som mest fanns det nog bortåt 25 personer som flätade korgar här i byn, berättar han. Men nu är det bara jag kvar.

Att bli en skicklig korgmakare är inte lätt. Det krävs tid och tålamod. Nu för tiden har folk ont om bådadera. Men det finns ändå några som vill försöka lära sig.

Svårt att klyva

— Det brukar komma några slöjdlärare från Alingsås, Floda och Lerum för att lära sig, säger Lennart. Att fläta korgarna är inte det svåraste. Svårigheten ligger i att klyva virket.

Lennart Petterssons korgar består av tunna, smala, långa list av gran och fur. Det är svårt att hitta rätt virke.

— Nu för tiden ska träden växa så fort för att skogen ska vara lönsam, och då blir det för långt mellan årsringarna och kvistar ända ner till roten, säger Lennart. Jag får hämta material från tre olika socknar i år. Det är svårt att hitta rätt träd. Riktigt säker är man inte förrän man har börjat klyva. Vill det sig illa får man hugga upp stocken till ved.

Vän med virket

Lennart Pettersson är vän med virket. Han klyver stockarna i allt tunnare längder. På de grövre styckena använder han en vanlig morakniv. Med lätta slag från ett vedträd driver han in kniven och bryter.

Han byter kniv. Precisionen skärps. Med en tunn slöjdkniv klyver han längderna tills han fått fram en längd med ungefär en kvadratcentimeters yta. Nu börjar det allra svåraste.

Ett snitt i änden frilägger årsringarna. Lennart skär försiktigt med kniven. Han för den fram och tillbaka, som om träet skulle få återhämta sig mellan varje tag. Via knivbladet känner han om virket gör motstånd.

En kniv om året

— Det går åt en morakniv om året ungefär, säger Lennart. Men jag har åtta stycken. Annars skulle jag få slipa för ofta. Så småningom ligger en hög med bågformade tunna lister vid hans fötter. De ska hyvlas innan det är dags att börja fläta. Hyveln är ett gammalt specialverktyg. Kanske hundra år gammalt.

I can see him standing at the gable of the barn, sharpening knives on the grindstone. Under the grindstone, there was a cut-off tyre of some kind that held water to wet it. Sometimes I got to crank the wheel of the stone, but it probably turned out better when he did it himself. There are many of these glimpses of memories left in my mind.

When I expressed a desire to learn what he did, grandad was puzzled. He didn't get angry but he was firm that I wouldn't, shouldn't, want to. Not because I was a girl, but because I didn't need to. Basketry was something you did because you needed money in your pocket, food on the table, and to supplement a meagre pension. He was born into a poor family, attended 'every other day school' for six years, then worked hard all his life on his own farm, as a casual labourer, as a day-labourer at the local sawmill, and as a basket maker. Furthermore, he and his family lived through two world wars.

When the local handicraft advisors later produced a film about the Hedared basket, starring himself in the main role, I think he felt some form of pride over his craftsmanship (at least I hope so). In any case, I thought it was fantastic. People came and filmed my grandfather, followed by a screening at the Borås Cultural Centre with a large audience in attendance. It must have been a significant moment for a tenant farmer from small Risa in Hedared.

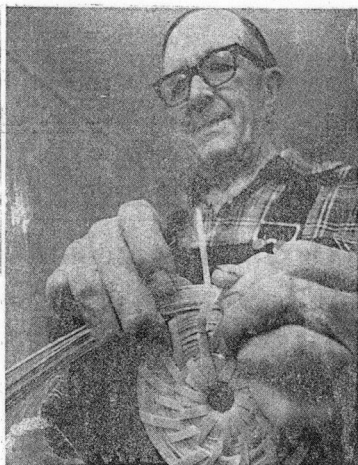

Grundkonstruktionen är den samma i Lennart Petterssons korgmodeller. En liten ring av tunna grenlister surras med Rhodans lister av järn. Ringarna, som grenlisterna kallas, surras sedan fast i vidare cirklar.

I didn't become a basket weaver as a child.

Later in life, I had a father-in-law who made baskets, Gustav Persson. He had learned to weave as a child but later found better means of survival. He resumed his basketry as a pensioner. He said that the knowledge was still in his body. I attended a few courses in making Hedared baskets with Gustav as my tutor, but gathering the material wasn't part of the course description. Felling trees in the forest was deemed beyond women's capabilities.

The nineties rolled around, with hard financial times, and I was unemployed. The Swedish state invented what was called 'ALU' jobs, roughly translated as 'Work Life Development' jobs. For six months, I received compensation to just weave baskets. Fantastic. A far cry from the hard labour of the 1920s that my grandfather was used to. But even during this time, we followed set gender patterns.
Gustav gathered the material, and I made the baskets. I got reasonably good at weaving baskets but not at gathering the material from scratch.

After this period, other work, studies, and children came along. Weaving baskets isn't like knitting. Once you start a basket, you have to finish it—it can't sit in a corner and wait for a month or two. Life came between me and the basketry, and my making was put on hold for over twenty years. In the meantime, Gustav got another apprentice, Curt Bengtsson, from Bollebygd (a neighbouring area close to Hedared). He turned out to be a natural despite enduring a lot of suspicion from Gustav in the first ten years of learning.

Today, Curt makes fantastic baskets and sells them in all corners of the world. He also teaches under the epithet 'the last basket maker' (to master the Hedared material technique). In one of his projects, 'The Hedared basket: then, now, later', he has gathered a group of artisans, practitioners who are very good at what they do—practitioners who have the needed abilities to learn the craft of the Hedared basket. My son Hannes (b. 1997) and I are included in this fantastic group. We have met and worked on all parts of the basket-making process for several weekends so far.

Even though I haven't made baskets in twenty years, the process still feels so familiar to my hands, and that makes me happy. When the wood splits along the annual rings in a straight line, it feels even better. Maybe I'll follow in Gustav's footsteps and resume this as a career when I retire.

Hannes and I are part of the project due to our roots in the soil, or perhaps just as village idiots. In any case, Hannes is of a determined, stubborn character and goes after what he wants, so who knows, maybe he's next in line to become 'the last basket maker' in Hedared. No pressure.

IN THEIR OWN WORDS

Hedare

On Thursday, 1 February 1968, an article in the local newspaper *Borås Tidning* had the headline 'Hedared baskets were sold across the Nordics: few basket makers maintain the tradition'. It presents Lennart in a time where there was 'seemingly no future for the craft', as someone who 'belongs to those that haven't given up'.

A clipping of the article, from its original edition, was first shown to me by Ulla Pettersson. It was when I later attended the Village Association's summer summit that I encountered it for a second time. I was there as a part of the meeting agenda, to present my research, and to meet the association in its entirety. The article was then presented by member Kent Schoultz, a local historical aficionado with deep family roots in the area.

> **What is important: I think the work has become more and more enjoyable over the years. It's something else now than when you toiled as a young boy until the skin broke.**
> **— Lennart Pettersson, 1968**

The spread features a photograph of Lennart working on what would soon become a basket, alongside another image of his cousin, and fellow basket maker, Oskar Johansson.

Oskar reflected on the unrelenting demands of making in the life of a Hedared basket maker, and when looking back, simply said: 'life has been work'.

During the period of the First World War (almost) the entire village made baskets, everyone, including young children, would help in the production of the basket. At the age of seven, Oskar made his first. When coming home from school,

s-korgar såldes över Norden

Fåtal korgmakare bevarar traditionen

Oskar Johansson på Skattegården i Hedared tar fram sina senast tillverkade korgar, flätade av gran eller furuspån med en teknik, som utbildades i Hedared och som man knappt finner nån annanstans i landet. Det är en sats om sex ostkorgar. Han får 54 kronor dussinet för dem. Timpengen blir inte stor, ett par kronor kanske.

Men händerna vill inte vila från ett arbete, som den snart 80-årige Oskar Johansson hållit på med sen han var nävaskar. För 70 år sen fick småknattar i Hedared lära sig "korga", innan de började skolan. Den lärdomen var viktig. Tidvis var korgmakandet huvudnäring på var och varannan gård i socknen.

Man tager ...

Ingen dag sjuk

Som pojke

Började 5-årig

Ingen framtid?

he would 'basket' until the evening rolled around. The family was paid two SEK per dussin.

167

When I was five years old, I was tasked with making the base of the basket. It wasn't deemed good enough to sell, but good for learning. It wore hard on a child's fingers, when cuts occurred, the only thing to do was to mend, and continue working.
— Lennart Pettersson, 1968

The article continues to describe how local merchants would come to Hedared and collect stock, to then sell the basket regionally and across Sweden—it even appeared in Norway and Finland. The marketplace often determined which designs were in fashion, and entire families would specialise in particular styles. Merchants would liaise with the client base, and makers like Lennart would then receive guidance on the types of baskets to produce.

'It is all one has learnt in one's day', says Oskar Johansson in his quiet way. But this 'all' happens to be an art, one that is still only known by a small number of people.

During the years of the Great Depression, Lennart describes how the village's basket making was affected by its hardships. Even if profitability slowly returned with time, the trade with merchants eventually began to diminish. As a result, a smaller range of designs was produced, leading to a greater uniformity in the types of baskets being made. Relying on crafting for a solid stream of income became increasingly difficult.

There seems to be no future for the craft. No one is continuing.

REVERENCE FOR THE DYING CRAFT

Fadhel [00:44:49] The basket must somehow be an extension of this place [the farm in Risa]. How important is Risa, is it more important than the basket itself?

> **Ulla [00:45:08]** The place is more important. The basket is also important, I would like to start basket making again but it's not a simple hobby, it's something you have to keep at.

Fadhel [00:45:36] What are your thoughts on if the basket were to disappear, with no one practising, what would happen to Hedared then?

> **Ulla [00:45:48]** That's how Gustav felt, that if no one makes baskets, the world will end. But it didn't.

Fadhel [00:45:57] But what will happen if no one practises? What do you think?

Korgflätningen är Hedareds stolthet

— Korghantverket måste vi värna om, menar Hedareds byaråd: Sture Sandblom, Bengt Andersson, Gösta Persson, Nils-Göran Nilsson, Thure Andersson och Jan Sandblom, här framför den gamla fattigstugan.

Foto: NILS HORNER

Hedareds egen specialitet och stolthet är korgar, av gran och av furu.

Förra århundradet fanns tillverkning i nästan varje stuga. Så sent som för fem år sedan slutade den sista korgflätaren.

Det är tveksamt om vi kan få någon efterföljare. Det här är en teknik som är så svår att lära att man nästan måste vara uppfödd med den för att behärska dem, säger Bengt Andersson, som sitter med i byarådet för Hedareds byalag.

Bengt är själv uppfödd med korgtillverkning i hemmet. Det var ett mycket vanligt sätt att dryga ut ekonomin för en småjordbrukare med många barn.

— Min far hade nio barn att försörja. Jag var med då många korgar blev till. Men själv kan jag inte konsten.

Ställer ut

I samband med att Hedareds byalag då tisdag mottar budkavlen för Hembygdens År, har rådet ställt i ordning en utställning om korgtillverkningen. Där kommer att finnas en rad olika korgmodeller och fotografier från olika tillverkningsställen.

En riktig Hedaredskorg ser ut på ett särskilt sätt, som bara en Hedaredsbo av äldre generation kan identifiera. I Bollebygd gjordes enekorgar. Men i Hedared gick man ut i skogen och letade efter gran och fur. Ibland kunde man få leta länge för att hitta virke med rätt "klöv".

— "Klöv" är ett uttryck för trästs beskaffenhet. För att kunna klyva furuspån krävdes både bra "agnaklöv" och "flaskaklöv", berättar Bengt Andersson.

Med det förra uttrycket menas trästs beskaffenhet på tvären över årsringarna. Det bestämde bredden på spånen. Det senare uttrycket står för tjockleken mellan årsringarna.

— Sedan skulle alltså virket klyvas med en mycket speciell teknik. Därefter flätades korgen med blöta spån.

Såldes i Göteborg

Vem som lärde Hedaredsborna denna intrikata teknik i början av 1800-talet vet man inte. Men plötsligt blev korgflätning en mycket vanlig binäring. Kommersen bedrevs i Göteborg dit tillverkarna själva åkte för att sälja sina alster.

— Men sedan kom det också uppköpare. Hedaredskorgarna såldes ända uppe i Gävle och även i Norge.

Bärkorgar i olika storlekar, tvättkorgar, brödkorgar, oat-

korgar, s k ystekorgar, konfektkorgar och blomsterkorgar. Modellerna är många liksom användningsområdena. Byalaget har en egen samling.

Liten förtjänst

Förtjänsten var inte så stor, kan det tyckas. Bengt Andersson berättar om en tillverkare som anslags mycket produktiv. Han gjorde ett dussin klädkorgar i veckan. För detta fick han på 1940-talet cirka 30 kronor.

Hedareds byalag består, som namnet avslöjar, av hela det lilla samhället.

— "Kollektivanslutning", skojar Thure Andersson som sitter med i rådet, vilket består av sex personer. Han erkänner sedan att aktiviteten utanför själva rådet är tämligen begränsad.

Få med ungdomar

— Vi hoppas förstås att det här med Hembygdens År ska få genomslagskraft. Det vore roligt att få med ungdomar också. Många har säkert inte en aning om hur viktig korgtillverkningen var för Hedared till exempel.

Huvudkvarter för byalaget är "sockenstugan". Det är ett gammalt fattighus från 1860-talet. Där visas på tisdagen korgutställningen.

— Korgarna är en viktig bit av Hedared. De är kultur och kultur ska spridas, understryker Bengt Andersson.

HELENE LUNDBOM

170

```
JAN ANDERSSON, CHAIRMAN
ULLA PETTERSSON, TREASURER
THE HEDARED VILLAGE ASSOCIATION

RISA, 02.22
```

FINDING THE WHY

Fadhel [00:23:42] What is the purpose of the Village Association? Why does the association exist?

> **Jan [00:23:47]** It exists to manage a donation that came from the old poor house that we had in the village. Three elderly men lived there, and when the last one passed away, he donated everything he owned to the village. There had to be an organisation in the village to take care of his estate, and that's how the Village Association was created, in the 1950s.

Fadhel [00:24:11] Where was the cottage located?

> **Jan [00:24:13]** The cottage is located at the furthest edge of the village, up east towards [the neighbouring village] Bredared, so far down in the parish that it wouldn't be noticed or seen by people in the village.

Fadhel [00:24:23] Do you know the name of the donor? Is he a known figure in the village?

> **Jan [00:24:30]** Yes, he is well known, Berglund. There were three Berglund brothers. In common speech, the parish cottage is called 'Berglund's'.

171

It was the Hedared municipality, as it was called back then, that was responsible for taking care of the poor or those who couldn't support themselves. So, all farms in the village had to chip in and contribute to make sure the parish cottage could be in operation and was well maintained. All farms jointly owned the cottage.

Two years ago, we compiled a list of the farms that had historically owned the parish cottage. Paying for the cottage was a form of municipal tax. When we went around to the previous owners, they all agreed to sign a 'Deed of Gift'. Through this, all the farms donated the cottage to the Village Association. The association is now the legal owner of the parish cottage.

Fadhel [00:26:26] So is the parish cottage renovated, or is it just an old run-down building?

Jan [00:26:29] We've kept it in order. It's in its original condition.

The parish cottage became a central point of reference when gathering material for the visuals of this body of research.

172

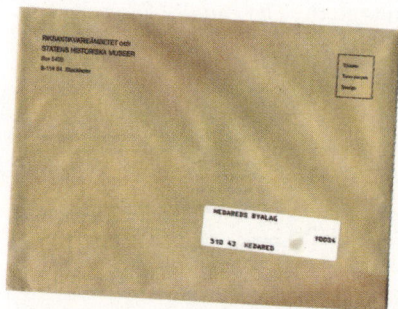

It acted in the same way as Lennart's farm in Risa—a physical space to anchor the collected stories. It is a treasure trove of artefacts, encompassing the village's history through the possessions of its former residents. The cottage contains utility items from the past two centuries, objects used and crafted by past villagers, alongside notes and documentation of the association's activities since its inception. Each thing holds its own narrative of bygone days.

I explored this rich collection (an archive in its own right), to document and gather source material, not only to contextualise but visualise:

What does the collective remembrance of a local craft heritage look like? Do memories differ from family to family?

Person to person? How does such a heritage inform the current self-image of a rural area?

How do these realities reflect the idea of belonging?

I was in need of visual cues that communicated the vastness of all my impressions, that embodied the anecdotes, histories and memories collected. I only needed to step through the door of the cottage to get a first glimpse of the rich material occupying its space. I sought what could act as renderings—things capturing the essence of a historical scene—objects or imagery needing no alteration, but only placement within the narrative of the research.

Adorning one wall in the parish cottage was *Budkavle*, a letter dispatched in 1984 by *Riksförbundet för Hembygdsvård.*

Its intended recipient: *The People of Sweden.*

The opening lines state:

> *In a tumultuous world with a threatening future,*
> *we shall come together, in freedom, to protect the values*
> *that shape human societies.*

safeguard the folk cultural heritage
counteract environmental decay
provide hembygdens youth with faith in the future
preserve and renew the traditions which
bring joy and comfort

Its direct translation reads in full:

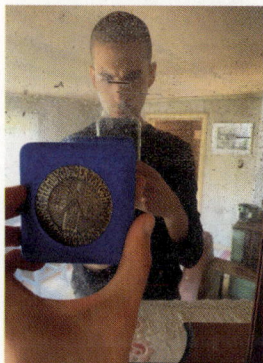

TILL SVERIGES FOLK

Budkavle kommer.
Den kallar till samling.

Så bars fordom bud genom svenska bygder
om fredligt arbete eller väpnad kamp.

1984, Hembygdens år, sändes återigen
budkavle genom landet.
Från en hembygd till en annan hembygd,
genom många hembygder skall den vandra.

Så lyder budkavlens ärende:
I en orolig värld med en hotfull framtid
skall vi gå samman för att i frihet värna de värden
som formar mänskliga samhällen.

Låt oss känna vårt ansvar genom att
- slå vakt om det folkliga kulturarvet
- motverka naturförstöring och miljöförfall
- ge hembygdens ungdom tro på framtiden
- bevara och förnya de traditioner som
ger glädje och trygghet.

Slut upp bakom hembygdsrörelsens strävan
att nå dessa mål!
Tillsammans skall vi kämpa för
våra gemensamma hembygder.

Därför vandrar budkavle genom landet att bestyrkas av
hembygdsförbund och hembygdsföreningar.

Budkavle har kommit. För den vidare!

På alla hembygdsvårdares vägnar
Riksförbundet för Hembygdsvård

TO THE PEOPLE OF SWEDEN

Budkavle is coming.
It calls for assembly.

Its message has travelled through Swedish bygder
of peaceful labour or armed fight.

1984, the year of Hembygden, budkavle is once again
sent through the country.
From one hembygd to another,
through many hembygder it shall wander.

Its message reads as follows:

In a tumultuous world with a threatening future,
we shall come together, in freedom, to protect the values
that shape human societies.

Let us know our responsibility by

* safeguard the folk cultural heritage
* counteract environmental decay
* provide hembygdens youth with faith in the future
* preserve and renew the traditions which
bring joy and comfort

Join the efforts of the hembygds movement
to achieve these goals!
Together we shall fight for
our common hembygder.

Budkavle wanders through the country, to be strengthened by
hembygdsförbund and hembygdsföreningar.

Budkavle has come. Pass it on!

On behalf of all hembygds custodians
Riksförbundet för Hembygdsvård

Känn Sjuhäradsbygden

There is no English equivalent to the word hembygd. The term consists of two words: *hem* (home) and *bygd*. The word bygd is defined as 'an inhabited area in the countryside that traditionally forms a unit based on historical, geographical, or economic reasons, often with emphasis on shared culture'.[1] Hembygd would roughly translate into 'one's native (home) district'.[2]

A hembygd simply refers to an area where a person has grown up or has lived in for a long time, and feels strong, life-long ties to; typically in reference to rural communities where the population is relatively stationary, but could nonetheless describe an area within a city.[3]

My hembygd would be Hulta, my mother's Hedared, and my father's Oulad Hamza.

Hembygdsrörelsen,[4] the hembygds movement, established itself at the turn of the twentieth century—a 'turbulent

178

time' defined by 'great societal changes'.[5] In short, the period was coloured by various organisations wanting to 'preserve traces from a disappearing culture'.[6] Today, local hembygds associations continue the work of preservation: to protect, share, and develop local cultural heritage. Typically run by volunteers, the activities of associations tend to be quite varied, reflecting local needs and interests. Associations can, for example, collectively maintain heritage centres: most of them open-air museums, hosting collections of historical buildings, or artefacts in extensive archives. Local associations are often affiliated with associations at the county level, and the larger umbrella organisation: the former *Riksförbundet för Hembygdsvård,* now known as *Sveriges Hembygdsförbund*—the Swedish Local Heritage Federation (founded in 1916).[7] Hembygdsrörelsen has over time expanded to include broader cultural and environmental concerns, by engaging in local community debates.

At the national level, the Federation often functions as a consultative body for various governmental committees.[8]

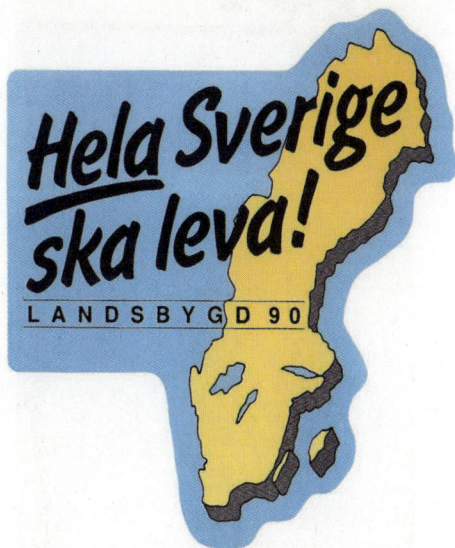

The direct translation of its 'ideological foundation' reads:

Hembygdsrörelsen is part of a living society. It builds bridges between the past, present, and future. The hembygds movement upholds a humanistic and democratic perspective. It is open to all, regardless of background. It respects the evolving forms of cultural heritage across space and time. Hembygds work fosters community, security, and identity. The interest in cultural heritage is the driving force behind a commitment to hembygden. Here, all generations meet.[9]

The historical trinkets sitting in the parish cottage contextualise the mission of Hembygdsrörelsen—to safeguard tradition and community identity. Other snippets of hembygds-history found in the cottage included documents sent to local associations; *byalag*, hembygdsförbund and hembygdsföreningar, also calling for gathering, labelled with the banner:

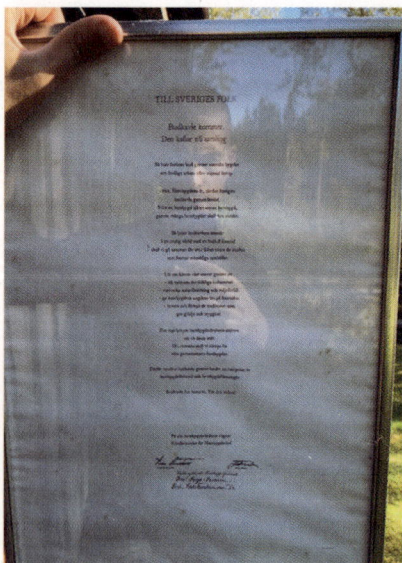

HELA SVERIGE SKA LEVA!
(ALL OF SWEDEN SHALL LIVE!)

'Hela Sverige ska leva' was founded in September 1989, at the end of a large campaign by the same name. This meant a strong mobilisation of Landsbygdssverige (rural Sweden) and after the campaign ended, local groups wanted to continue to work together to develop their villages and communities. That was the start of a long journey towards a country in balance. A journey that is still underway.[10]

UPPROP! was the headline of a letter dispatched from the same sender, as part of the same campaign.

Its message reads:

UPPROP!

The Swedish society is changing. Metropolitan areas are growing stronger today than they have for a long time. Simultaneously, many people are moving from smaller cities, communities, and landsbygd. Our open agricultural landscape is growing shut, and many plant and animal species are endangered. This development is not good for landsbygden—it is not good for *stads*bygden either.

More than 90 folkrörelser with 70.000 associations are now cooperating in a *Nationell folkrörelsekommitté* together with authorities and industry to reverse this trend. Hela Sverige ska leva! is our common slogan.

All forces must now gather to preserve a living bygd and nature. A strong public opinion is necessary for a majority to realise the consequences of the transition that is now taking place, and to actively ensure that hela Sverige ska leva.

We therefore urge all of Sweden's associations in different bygder and communities:
— form local bygde-committees
— start study groups
— adopt programmes and make statements concerning bygden's problems and opportunities.

It's about the future of your bygd.

Ingemar Mundebo
Ordf. i Nationella Folkrörelsekommittén

UPPROP!

Det svenska samhället förändras. Storstadsregionerna växer idag starkare än på länge. Samtidigt flyttar många människor från mindre städer, orter och landsbygd. Vårt öppna odlingslandskap växer igen och många växt- och djurarter är hotade. Den utvecklingen är inte bra för landsbygden — den är inte bra för stadsbygden heller.

Mer än 90 folkrörelser med 70.000 föreningar samverkar nu i en Nationell folkrörelsekommitté tillsammans med myndigheter och näringsliv för att vända den utvecklingen. Hela Sverige ska leva! är vår gemensamma paroll.

Alla krafter måste nu samlas för att bevara en levande bygd och natur. En stark opinion är nödvändig för att alla människor ska inse konsekvenserna av den omvandling som nu pågår och aktivt verka för att hela Sverige ska leva.

Vi uppmanar därför alla Sveriges föreningar i olika bygder och orter:

— att bilda bygdekommittéer

— att starta studiecirklar

— att anta program och göra uttalanden som rör bygdens problem och möjligheter.

Det handlar om framtiden för din bygd.

Ingemar Mundebo
Ordf. i Nationella Folkrörelsekommitén

Today, Hela Sverige ska leva (English translation: Rural Sweden) is a nationwide, non-profit organisation whose membership consists of thousands of community groups, councils and associations, dedicated to local development.
At the national level, its operations aims to synthesise the needs of its local branches, and 'act as a collective voice of the rural movement in Sweden.'[11]

Its (slightly condensed) manifesto reads:

LANDSBYGDSUTVECKLING I ÄLVSBORGS LÄN
Nr 88:2

ÄLVSBORGS LÄNS BUDKAVLAR

Många av länets byalag och föreningar har deltagit i den budkavlekedja som cirkulerat i länets 18 kommuner under tiden april till augusti.

De byalag och föreningar som deltagit i budkavlekedjan har lämnat idéer, krav och synpunkter på hur landsbygden skall levandegöras. Många har även skrivit under Landshövding Göte Fridhs apell om större resurser till underhåll av det allmänna vägnätet i Älvsborgs län.

I de synpunkter som framkommit finns en stor samstämmighet mellan länets kommuner. Många av de krav och idéer som framförs är allmänt hållna, men de visar på problem och möjligheter som går att utveckla.

De vikrigaste problemformuleringarna är:

* Kommunikationer
* Boende- boendeservice
* Miljö
* Näringsliv/sysselsättning
* Utbildning - kultur - fritid
De inkomna förslagen sammanställdes till en länssammanfattning som överlämnads på Skansen den 28 augusti.

Här följer några axplock ur mängden av krav och idéer:

KOMMUNIKATIONER

"Goda kommunikationer är av stor betydelse för en levande landsbygd. Det gäller el - tele - vdg - vatten och luftförbindelser. Dessa

kommunikationer är viktiga för livet i en glesbygd i synnerhet. Det kan liknas vid blodomloppets betydelse för cellens utveckling". Torrskogs byalag.

* Större resurser till upprustning av de mindre allmänna vägarna.

"Att vägstandarden överlags höjs, så att vägarna är farbara under hela året". Byalaget i Järbo.

* Tele och eliedningar bör hålla god standard. Bevara postservicen på landsbygden.

LÄNSSTYRELSEN
ÄLVSBORGS LÄN
462 82 Vänersborg
0521 - 70 000

Hans Persson   0521 - 70164

Barbro Holmberg 0521 - 70155

Lars-Erik Larsson
Lantbruksnämnden
Box 1147 462 28 Vänersborg
0521 - 12080

Our goal is simple. We want to have balance between the country-side and city.

We will achieve this balance when rural areas are treated fairly, i.e. they are given development opportunities equivalent to those provided to urban areas. [...] The solutions are not necessarily going to be the same for rural areas as for urban areas. Instead, solutions should be adapted to the conditions and needs in a given place. Rural areas have to develop on their own terms.

Now we are touching on an important point, and that is how rural areas are viewed.

Today, there is a widely-held urban norm that views cities and towns as where modern life is lived, and where creativity and innovative thinking flourish, with the people in rural areas and villages portrayed as the opposite, i.e. as back-ward-looking and static.

We want to contribute to ending this myth and to fostering a more multifaceted and equitable portrayal of our rural areas.

We hope that this work can lead to a better distribution of re-sources between the countryside and city and to a greater under-standing of the important contribution rural areas make to all of Sweden's development.

When there is a balance between the countryside and the city, then we will have achieved our vision where
Hela Sverige Ska Leva. [12]

*Hela Sverige Ska Leva Sjuhärad is perhaps more
important than ever. With a new surrounding
world, with new challenges and new opportunities, our organisation has a very important role to
play. We work for a country in balance, to create
equal opportunities in being able to live and reside
throughout the country, and for everyone to
be included.*[13]

Naturally, in line with such principles is the Hedared Village
Association, whose purpose is to govern the interests aris-
ing in the village—keeping an eye on the past, whilst sharply
keeping its gaze on the future. A recent example of their work
that reflects the nature of the organisation is the association's
brochure, 'Hedaredsbygden: Local Economic Analysis—a tool
for development'.

This small booklet single-handedly ignited my interest
to work with the Village Association, and to continue researching the origins of the basket. It, too, much like the finds in the
parish cottage, gave new additions to the patchwork.

Its content formed the talking points for my initial
conversation with the Village Association, when I spoke with
their Chairman, Jan. It summarises the village, filtered through
the mission of the association: who they were, are, and wish to
become.

It includes a series of brief historical facts:

*In the cadastral survey, enacted in 1849–1852, it states
that the village consists of 9 farms whose names are still in
use today: Eriksgården, Gårdsfogdegården, Haraldsgården,
Larsagården, Skattegården, Älvsgården, Risa, Granholmen,
and Ingeshult.

*A large part of the area is woodland, overgrown with
spruce and fir. Forestry has provided income alongside the
mostly smaller farms:
*Where the plough cannot go, and the scythe cannot strike,
is where the tree shall stand.*

LANDSBYGDSUTVECKLING I ÄLVSBORGS LÄN

Hela Sverige ska leva!

18 BUDKAVLAR FRÅN ÄLVSBORGS LÄN

EN SAMMANFATTNING

AFFÄR
KULTUR
ÄLDREVÅRD
SKOLA
VÄGAR
BARNOMSORG
SJUKVÅRD
ARBETE
FRITID

LÄNSSTYRELSEN
ÄLVSBORGS LÄN
462 82 Vänersborg
0521 - 70 000

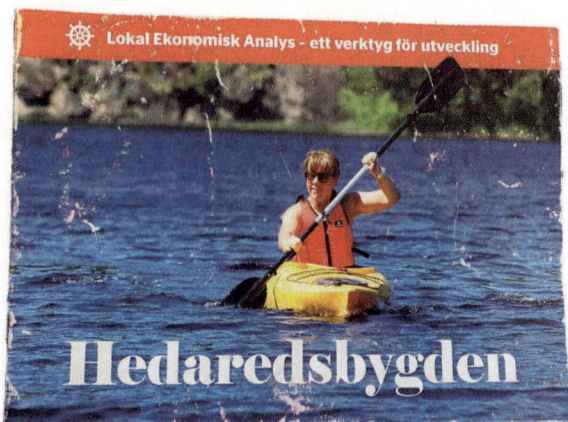

Lokal Ekonomisk Analys - ett verktyg för utveckling

Hedaredsbygden

*Sweden's only preserved stave church is located in the village, whose timber has been dated from between 1498 to 1503. Part of the church, and objects found inside of it, indicate that another church had been in the village during the 1200s or even the 1100s.

Before listing these historical facts, it opens to say:

Between the design city of Borås and the café city of Alingsås lies Hedared, along with the surrounding area we call Hedaredsbygden. *Situated at just the right distance from shopping, restaurants, and vibrant nightlife, we strive to create a safe place where everyone can feel welcome.*

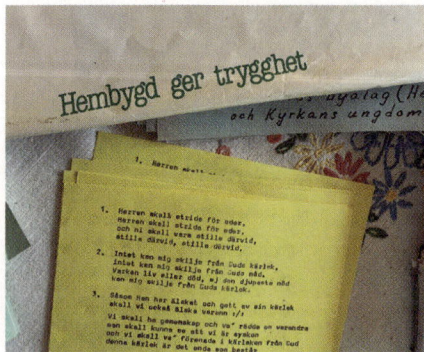

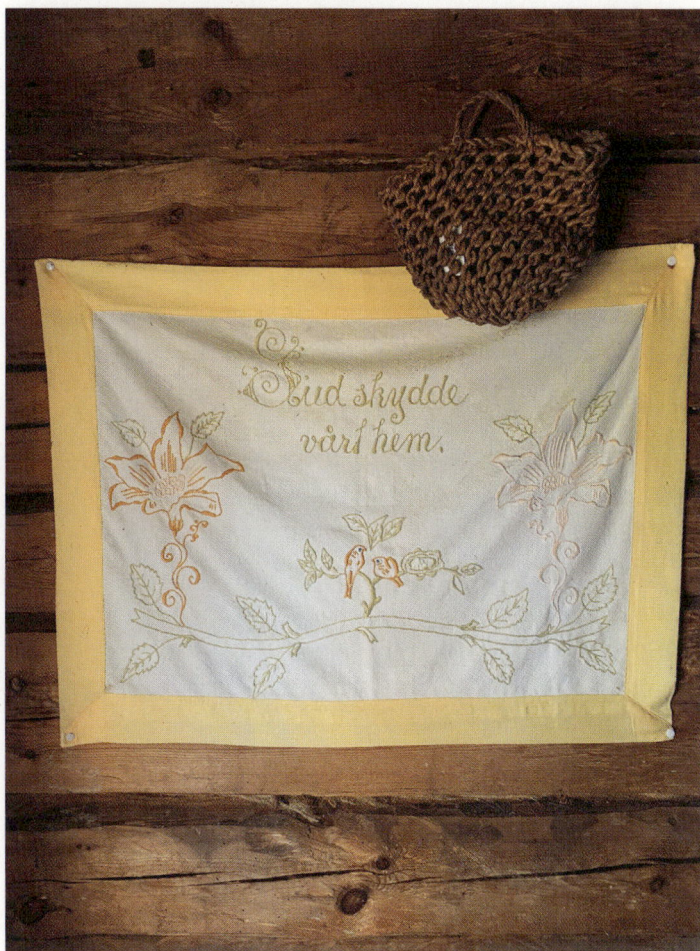

The Village Association simply continues to be an embodiment of the hembygds movement's mission—striving towards a future in which Hela Sverige Ska Leva.

Fadhel [00:50:08] What does Hedared mean to you?

> **Ulla [00:50:13]** It's my home. I can very well imagine living in other places in the world. I have nothing against moving away from here, but this is my home. This is where I belong [at the farm in Risa].
> However, I wouldn't want to live down in the village.

Fadhel [00:50:49] Is there a difference between Risa and 'down in the village' [Hedared]?

> **Ulla [00:50:53]** ...I grew up in the centre of the village in the 60s, when all the mothers were housewives... It was very lively on Källstigen... We built our house there in '65.

Fadhel [00:51:38] How does it feel when you drive by now? What I see when looking at the house is the balcony fence on the first floor, the one grandad made at the sawmill. Its shape feels so typical grandad to me. Otherwise, the house looks the same [since being bought and now has new owners], was it also brown when you lived there [growing up]?

Ulla [00:52:01] Its facade was covered in chemical panels. Lethal panels.

Fadhel [00:52:09] That feels very of its time, the 60s-70s.

Ulla [00:52:13] But it was great. It was cheap.

Fadhel [00:16:00] Where in the village did you grow up?

Jan [00:16:02] I grew up in the 'village centre'. I grew up in the only rental property at the time, where I spent my early years. I was six years old when we moved to our house, which my father built, and then I lived there until around the time of my military service, after I moved away for several years, before coming back around 1980.

Fadhel [00:16:36] Why did you come back? Was it an obvious choice?

Jan [00:16:38] My brother and I bought our grandfather's old farm. We were involved in sheep farming already, so my brother, myself, and my father (who was alive at the time), worked together on this farm. Back then I didn't live too far away from Hedared. We moved back so we could be closer to the animals: we had both sheep and horses for a while, and so my children grew up nearby.

Fadhel [00:17:11] But the farm was more of a hobby business?

Jan [00:17:16] Yes, exactly. I spent a lot of time on the family farm when I was growing up, help-ing my uncle at that time with harvesting and such. Most kids were involved in that, and when my uncle retired, there was an opportunity to buy the farm and the land around it, so my

191

brother and I did, and we've had it ever since. We've worked in the forest together for forty-two years. So it's been quite an adventure.

Fadhel [00:17:58] When you mention working in the forest... What does that entail?

Jan [00:18:00] It means doing everything, from final felling to all the rest—we're simply out cutting down trees.

Fadhel [00:18:07] And selling the timber?

Jan [00:18:08] And selling directly, yes. We do the final felling and we do all the other processes in the forest too.

Fadhel [00:18:28] For someone completely new to forestry, what do these processes involve?

Jan [00:18:37] It goes like this: you own forest land... In the 1840s a cadastral survey was done here. After it was completed, the survey formed farms in the order of magnitude 'just over a hundred hectares'. Many farms were affected by the fact that there were often two sons who had to share the farm, and farms began to decrease in size to fifty hectares, and it turned out that those fifty-hectare farms you could actually live off. From the end of the nineteenth century until around the mid-1960s, a family could live fairly well on a fifty-hectare farm. Then agriculture became unprofitable, and people had to look for other industries.

Fadhel [00:19:31] Why couldn't you turn a profit?

Jan [00:19:32] On average [in Hedared], you maybe had four or five cows, and possible milk production from those who had dairy cows. Then, some people had a few more self-sufficient chickens. You had pigs, all of which were for self-sustenance, but this wasn't enough to sustain yourself and make a living from it. So most people started working in industry, at Sand & Betong etc. These farms then became hobby farms with casual agricultural land instead. The farm was my father's childhood home... In my youth, it was always in the periphery. The younger generation that was supposed to take over realised that it didn't work to survive solely on farming, so 'now I have to get a job'. I became an engineer and worked with that my whole professional life.

Fadhel [00:20:38] In relation to the forest?

Jan [00:20:40] I ran a consultancy firm in the HVAC industry, and that was my job during normal working hours. In my spare time, I worked physically with my body. Now, I need to explain one more thing about forest work: planning. You make a ten-year plan and you get help to do that [from the Swedish Forest Agency]. A forestry plan simply outlines ten years ahead in time, essentially describing 'these are the things we are going to do'. That plan relates to both timber production and the 'natural values' [the preservation of the land].

Fadhel [00:21:23] How has it evolved from when you started until now?

193

Jan [00:21:27] The processes in the forest have evolved from being purely production-oriented to focusing on 'important production' and the conservation of 'natural values' has also come into consideration more and more.

Fadhel [00:21:38] What do 'natural values' mean?

Jan [00:21:40] It means that you set aside, for example, five percent of the forest land for reserves. You can't do anything with it. You just have to let it be just as it is. Another five percent should be actively conserved and taken care of, for example, growing birch groves, keeping them tidy, and making sure the conditions are right for birch trees to continue to thrive and grow there.

Fadhel [00:22:02] Making sure you remove weeds?

Jan [00:22:05] You remove spruces and make sure deciduous trees survive. You should take care of watercourses. You are not allowed to cut down trees along watercourses, etc.

Fadhel [00:22:18] You should simply follow the rules?

Jan [00:22:20] It is largely based on different certifications, a forestry certification [when selling your timber] that says 'the timber we deliver comes from sustainable forestry that takes nature into account', which in turn is the argument when selling on the European market: 'This is not a clear-cut forest but well-utilised, well-looked-after forest'.

Fadhel [00:26:59] And then, regarding this brochure, I thought about how it says 'positive forces working together', '...we wish to form a safe place where everyone feels welcome'. What does this project mean for the Village Association and Hedared at large?

Jan [00:27:16] Essentially, it's about increasing the population in Hedared. There are many ways to do this, but we want to do it by building more houses, by exploiting the municipal land in Hedared that's available for residential construction. That's why we wanted to create a brochure that tells people it's pretty nice to be able to move and to live here in Hedared. Naturally, we only emphasise things in this brochure that are the advantages of living in this village. That's why there are many phrases attached to the village's identity, we want people to move here... If you work at Volvo and commute from Gothenburg, you should strongly consider moving to Hedared and stop commuting. There's a lot about this that permeates the brochure.

Fadhel [00:28:17] Are there any values that could summarise Hedared?

Ulla [00:28:37] Many of us pretty much agree that it's nature, the forest, that unites us.

Jan [00:28:48] Yes, of course. That's the common value. It's the value of nature and what's in the forest. In the village, there's not too much crime or anything... I see the downsides of living here too, of course, but there's no reason to highlight those in the brochure... We want to highlight the positive aspects. Just like in the choice of image on the front page, it should be fun, to show that things are 'happening' here.

Fadhel [00:29:26] What would be the downside of living here?

Jan [00:29:34] Well, maybe, in the past, there was more of a community life, more people were involved. Today—

Ulla [00:29:41] There were more volunteers before.

Jan [00:29:43] Yes, today, many people don't want to get involved, and have a rather simplified view of life.

Fadhel [00:29:55] There's not so much focus on community?

Jan [00:29:58] It's not as present as it used to be.

Fadhel [00:30:01] Why do you think that is?

Jan [00:30:06] I think because the population in general, people in general, don't have the same interests they used to have in the past... They just aren't as engaged.

Fadhel [00:30:41] Do you think that's something typical of the present day?

Jan [00:30:51] I think there's a connection there. The younger generation has had an easier upbringing, unlike Lennart, who started working at home and learning to appreciate things at the age of twelve. Today, the community is no longer at the forefront.

Fadhel [00:31:33] If we go back to the forest... Regarding the construction the brochure is promoting, when you're talking about the forest, if I understand it correctly, is there municipal land where this construction is meant to happen? In keeping with their forestry plan, would construction not disturb the biodiversity, if the forest is to be removed, or is it allocated for construction?

Jan [00:32:04] There's a little nook there. The municipal land is two hectares in size. It was once bought by the old municipality and was later merged into the current Borås municipality. An inventory of the land has been conducted, indicating that there's a bit of old spruce forest there. This was a find confirmed at the county level. I've discussed this with them, and their response was: 'Whilst we've indeed established [that there's a section of old spruce forest], it has not been reserved or earmarked to be preserved in any way. We have simply confirmed that there is such a forest here'. So you're right that there's a small 'sharp corner' here, which is not contentious, but potentially a bit problematic.

Fadhel [00:33:14] Me and Ulla were talking about this, that when you clear woodland, anyone can oppose it, it's an open forum.

Ulla [00:33:24] Yes, that if you were to fell woodland, someone, anyone, even up in north Sweden could ob-

197

ject to it, and if it's done with good reason, it has to be looked into by the Swedish Forest Agency.

Fadhel [00:33:37] With this new development project, to what extent has the village been involved? Have you had meetings? Has there not been a significant engagement there as well?

Jan [00:33:50] We kicked off with a digital town hall meeting. Several folks joined, this was during the pandemic, and we decided to form a group to draft a budget, collect data about public opinion etc., and then disseminate the information to both the management team of the Village Association working on this, and a secondary support group. I then reached out to those villagers who showed interest from the beginning and informed them about our progress. The idea is to gather in person for another town hall meeting and tie up any loose ends. There's very limited data from SCB [Statistics Sweden], so we only have a very limited amount of statistics that can be reported... Coompanion Sjuhärad has been helping us with this project and has also been [part of these meetings] to talk generally about what they do in these matters.

Fadhel [00:35:04] They support cooperative development?

Jan [00:35:07] Yes, and they operate at the county level. So anyone in the village can come and participate in this.

Fadhel [00:35:29] Is there slightly more engagement among a specific age group?

Jan [00:35:36] The goal is for as many people as possible to be involved. It will likely be predominantly an older audience, as one might imagine.

Fadhel [00:35:56] And how far away is the development from actually happening?

Jan [00:36:00] We are trying to interest two [potential partners]. Partly it is the municipality and then the local housing company. We have to build a credible market for this, and that's why we have surveyed it. It asked questions about how [people want to live] and what type of housing people are looking for, but we got back too few responses from the villagers...

Fadhel [00:37:00] Asking what types of housing the majority would like to live in?

Jan [00:37:02] Yes, housing that is slightly differently designed, we're quite confident that [the villagers] would want some kind of elderly-adapted housing, catering to the older members in the community.

Ulla [00:37:12] Because the idea is to build smaller places, so people can transition from their larger houses?

Jan [00:37:20] Yes, but can you imagine, if you sit down to engage with things like this, and you have to fill out [a form] and imagine what your needs would be [as someone older] in five years, when you may not be able to live in your own home anymore... It can be a hard thing to do.

Fadhel [00:37:47] We've talked about agriculture and briefly mentioned the cottage industry that Lennart was a part of. The two are very much intertwined and were on the decline when the local industry [Volvo Proving Ground and Sand & Betong] appeared in the village... How important has access to reliable employment been in Hedared, from then to now, with a company like Sand & Betong?

Jan [00:38:26] When agriculture wasn't enough to live on, you had to find another source of income, and it's very fortunate that there was an industry to turn to. There were more examples than basket making as a supplement to the old farming life. You also had knitting, which was done at home for the local textile industry [part of the cottage industry in the Seven Districts]. My aunt sat and knitted with a knitting machine in her home... The basket making occurred in many places. I'm sure you've checked out many different places, and seen all the different products that were made. Some were specialists in certain things. Like Lill-Oskar's mangle baskets, these fantastic creations. I experienced it live and sat with Lill-Oskar [as a child] while he made them.

Fadhel [00:39:32] Who's Lill-Oskar?

Jan [00:39:35] Lill-Oskar was a lovely character... He lived opposite the parish hall, in a big yellow house with his wife Alva... He made a living from his baskets, he had nothing else.

Fadhel [00:39:53] During what years was this?

Jan [00:39:58] He might have passed away around '69.

Ulla [00:40:01] I remember him, and I was born in '65.

Jan [00:40:05] Yes, he couldn't have been much older than seventy. I don't recall him having any other job. He had several specialities but his mangle baskets are the most well-known.

Fadhel [00:40:47] When it comes to Sand & Betong, Volvo... Do they have any significance for the community at large, does each company have a specific meaning? Is either company more valuable to the community?

Jan [00:41:04] Sand & Betong have had a significant impact.

Ulla [00:41:09] You can think of it like this: I was born on the street Källstigen. On Källstigen, there was Rune Holm, he had his own construction company. Then everyone else worked at Sand & Betong. My dad worked there, [the neighbours] Sven-Erik, Henry,

K-G, and in the terraced houses [on the same street]: Fadhel's grandfather Stig worked there, although he was a bit unfaithful and took similar jobs elsewhere... It wasn't until Volvo helped to build all these new houses, essentially building Munk Road and Kloster Road [in the centre of Hedared], that the village felt an influx of [new] people, mainly from Gothenburg.

Jan [00:41:50] That was the historical side to things, of course, but if we think about it today, how much Volvo affects the cohesion in the village, it's not so much... Some villagers work there and that's it. It's nothing compared to Sand & Betong, which has had such a strong influence on the village's development throughout its operations.

Fadhel [00:42:13] In the community spirit, its part of it?

Jan [00:42:14] Yes, and practically too, Sand & Betong run the grocery store in the village. Let me give you a better example: I have a snowmobile, now, the weather is not often ideal to use it, but I got it because Kjell-Åke and I were planning to make ski tracks along the hiking trails in the village.

Fadhel [00:42:25] Who's Kjell-Åke?

Jan [00:42:27] Let's just say he's one of the crowd... So, we found some photos of a track sled, and were considering building one ourselves. So, I emailed Kjell-Åke the drawings, and he printed them out at Sand & Betong, where he worked. Then Bertil, the manager at Sand & Betong, came and asked him: 'What's this all about?' Kjell-Åke explained that we were thinking of building a track sled for this and that reason. Bertil then immediately said: 'Interesting, we'll buy that!' So, Sand & Betong sent two men up to Dalarna [in Northern Sweden] to buy a track sled for us to be able to make these ski tracks. That's how they thought... I even got petrol money to then lay the actual tracks. It's in the little things that [Sand & Betong] think about the village.

Fadhel [00:43:58] So they always think, 'village first'?

Jan [00:44:02] They are extremely important for the community. There's no doubt.

Fadhel [00:44:08] And do the owners live in the village?

Jan [00:44:11] Yes.

Fadhel [00:44:12] Is it family-owned?

Ulla [00:44:16] Yes, I think it was Göran's father, or Göran himself who started it all, and he had three children.

Jan [00:44:26] Göran and his brother Erik were the ones who started it. Then the family continued, and they have done a lot for the village.

Fadhel [00:44:43] They have deep roots here?

Jan [00:44:44] Very much so.

FAMILY LAND

```
LENA GUSTAVSSON
DAUGHTER OF GÖRAN SAMUELSSON
(FOUNDER OF SAND & BETONG)

TELEPHONE INTERVIEW, 06.22
```

Lena (b. 1948), stands among pine trees that she and her father Göran, founder of the local concrete factory, Sand & Betong, planted seven decades ago. These trees, as old as the Hedared Village Association itself, still grace the land that belongs to her family.

> *My brother lives right across from where they were planted. I look out at them sometimes and wonder where the time has gone. My father wrote about it in his journal. Dad wrote 'to his little Lena'.*

Fadhel [00:23:09] One thing I immediately think of when we mention agriculture is, of course, the forest. What has the forest meant to you during your upbringing? Has your relationship with it changed from when you were young?

> **Lena [00:23:24]** One thing that comes to mind is when my father and I were in the forest that belonged to us. It might have been 1952-54. Then he said to me: 'Now you are going to come with me, we're going to plant some pine trees up on the pasture hill', and they're very tall now, I can tell you that.

Fadhel [00:23:50] So you know exactly which trees were the ones you planted?

Lena [00:23:55] My brother lives right across from where they were planted. I look out at them sometimes and wonder where the time has gone. My father wrote about it in his journal. Dad wrote 'to his little Lena'.

Fadhel [00:24:37] One last question—is there any object, item, or place in the village that symbolises Hedared for you? I'm thinking it might be the place where those trees are.

Lena [00:25:11] Yes, that would be it.

Pine is now the primary material used in the Hedared basket. Due to its resin-rich properties, pine can be bent into shape, allowing it to take on the forms used in basket making. Typically, trees 'mature' between eighty to one hundred years before they are considered suitable for 'harvesting', and ready to be used as material.

A PLACE CALLED HOME

Fadhel [00:46:12] When it comes to places to gather, like the parish cottage, the parish hall etc... How important are they?

Jan [00:46:29] Both are important gathering places for meetings... We have meetings with the Village Association in both. Most recently, many was held at the parish hall... We started some archival work which is also located in the parish hall.

Fadhel [00:47:04] What does that entail?

Jan [00:47:06] It means that there was a pandemic as is well known, during which we bought some equipment; a scanner, boxes and some other stuff, and started to prepare the framework for our archive, how it will work, and what will be part of it.

Fadhel [00:47:40] What is it made up of? Pictures?

Jan [00:47:43] Pictures, documents, written records.

Fadhel [00:47:45] Collected from residents?

Jan [00:47:47] Yes, so we've started with that. We have to get started properly, to first know how we should handle it. We have a lot [of material] on the shelf to document. That's why we have a site called Hedared.se. It's not in use today, but the domain is taken. The idea is that we use all the functionality available online, and store all our archival material there, so anyone can access it by simply visiting Hedared.se.

Fadhel [00:48:48] So it's for the history of the village?

Jan [00:48:51] We have divided it into two main categories: buildings and personalities. We have for example talked about making one for the most prominent figures in the village. One being Göran Samuelsson [founder of Sand & Betong]. He has written a text about his own and his father Edvard's story. About their life's work. It's fantastically well-written.

Fadhel [00:49:26] So will that be something available on the site?

Jan [00:49:29] Yes, that could be an example. Another is 'John from Lindhem', who was also known as a basket maker. He had a hobby of writing hymns, without success, I would argue. Regardless, he wrote these hymns, and the priest in the village went through his hymns to find out in relation to what these texts could possibly be drawn from. A bit odd, but it's fun material. So there's a lot to it.

Lena [00:01:11] I have these notes... My dad has written a bit about his life. Would any of it resonate with your work?

Fadhel [00:01:24] Yes, perhaps.

Lena [00:01:26] It's been fifteen years since he passed away. I sometimes read his stories. It's quite something to read, but you can borrow it. Dad wrote it in his 'twilight years' after he retired. He reflects on how life was back then with his dad and brothers and such, it goes back quite far in time. Dad was the youngest child in his family. But then grandad was the youngest in that family, out of 14 siblings. So it's a really strange family in that way. Dad managed to talk a lot about the family. We got to listen to so many stories, luckily we had grandma in the house so you could go to her when you got tired of him...

Fadhel [00:03:29] It must have been quite uncommon for a man from that generation to talk so much about the past?

Lena [00:03:33] He was a very unusual sight.

Fadhel [00:03:35] When I think of my grandad... He was a very kind, but a very quiet man.

Lena [00:03:47] Dad probably found it a bit hard to keep quiet, so it's different, but it meant that we've heard many stories.

Fadhel [00:03:59] I think it's quite important to know where you come from, to feel secure in your family roots, when you know where you come from, you know where you're going in some way.

> **Lena [00:04:07]** It can be a bit smoother sailing or more secure sailing, that's for sure, knowing that they were there.

Fadhel [00:04:13] In short, think this project has a lot to do with looking back in order to move forward.

> **Lena [00:04:26]** Then I believe these [texts] can be really beneficial.

***

Lena's father Göran was, alongside his brother Erik, one of the founders of the concrete factory HEDA Sand & Betong located in the village. Founded in 1952, its presence in Hedared meant, for the villagers, access to stable employment, and for the factory, a loyal workforce right on its doorstep. The factory, in its seventy-third year of operation, still has its headquarters in Hedared, and still today, is run by the founding family.

The notes mentioned by Lena refer to what could be described as Göran's memoirs. At the age of 66, he states in the opening paragraphs that, as a pensioner with time on his side, he intends to go back as far as he remembered:

> Reciting my own memories, and the stories of
> people I have met during the journey through life.
> I hope my description will correspond with facts
> as closely as possible.

Written on a typewriter, commenced on 12 February 1990, Göran's story begins with a reflection on his family, tracing his lineage back to his father's life and business-related endeavours. He explains how his family were not basket makers themselves, their focus was on managing the production of wooden boxes for the fishing industry. Göran ran a sawmill that procured such wood for sale. However, fluctuating pricing variables and uncertain profit margins led him to seek a more financially stable industry for his growing family. This pursuit resulted in a partnership with his brother Erik, and together they founded Sand & Betong in the 1950s.

Spanning 34 pages, the text concludes on 2 November 1993 saying:

What's Hedared like these days?

In the early 70s, around twenty houses were built in Hedared due to Volvo constructing a test track in the nearby area. The test drivers wanted to settle in the village. This has become a positive element and most of the families have now become integrated here. There have also been around twenty new terraced rental flats developed in recent years. This is good for the village, as its older population, who can't take care of their house and garden, have sold it to the next generation, and instead opted to rent a flat. There, life can hopefully continue for a few years, with more ease.

***

I think Hedared is a small, but wonderful place to have spent one's life in.

Jag föddes 1924. Idag är det den 12 febr. 1990. Jag har hunnit
med att fylla 66 år och är pensionär med tiden på min sida.
Därför tänker jag nu gå tillbaks i tiden så långt jag kan för
att förmedla egna minnen, samt berättelser från människor jag
mött under färden genom livet. Jag hoppas min förmedling skall
överensstämma med fakta så nära som möjligt.

Familjen jag kom till 1924 bestod av pappa Josef Edvard
Samuelsson, mamma Rut Sofia, födda 1880 resp. 1896. 3 st
halvbröder, Erik Natanael född 1907, Algot Samuel född 1908,
Konrad Valfrid född 1913. Göta min helsyster född 1921. Mina
bröders mamma Almina dog 1918 då spanska sjukan spred död i
bygderna i trakterna här.

Vi bodde på en liten gård, Älvsgården 5:3, i Hedared. Denna
födde 3 st kor samt i regel 2 st grisar. Detta att ha tillgång
till mjölk och fläsk samt möjlighet att odla potatis och
spannmål var nästan en nödvändighet för att kunna överleva på
landsbygden vid den tiden, eftersom en svår tid med
arbetslöshet, svält och depression rådde i Sverige liksom i hela
Europa och Amerika efter första världskriget som slutat något år
innan. Dessa svåra tider fanns kvar ända tills år 1936-37.
Möjligheterna att få in kontanta pengar var små. Familjerna hade
dock en stor press på sig för helt utan kontanter gick inte att
leva även om det för 5-10 kronor blev så mycket varor att mor i
huset nått och jämt orkade bära hem dessa. Hemma hos oss satt
familjemedlemmarna tidvis och stickade tröjor, strumpor, vantar
mm. med maskiner som lånades ut från företag i Borås. Dessa
tillhandahöll garn varför det var fråga om arbeslöner. Denna låg
väldigt lågt. Det gick nog bara att tjäna 1.00 - 1.50 per dag.

I Hedared förekom vid denna tid även korgtillverkning. Dessa
flätades av familjemedlemmarna i något stort rum eller i köket i
boningshuset. Det fanns uppköpare i byn. Dessa skickade alstren
med järnväg över hela Sverige. Dessa duktiga korgmakare tjänade
något bättre med pengar än övriga arbetare.

Det hade byggts ett vattenkraftverk omkring år 1915, ovanför
Västra Valsjön (Hansasjön) vid ån som kommer ut från Forsabäcken
till Nolån. Detta betjänade hela Hedared, utom Risa. Kapaciteten
var väldigt låg och kraftverket var avsett att leverera ljus för
byn då kriget medfört besvärligheter att få fram fotogen till
dåtida lampor. Det gick inte att använda strykjärn eller värme-
element för då slocknade lamporna. Kraftverket startades på
eftermiddagen när det började skymma, stannades kl. 22.30 på
kvällen för att startas kl. 5.30 på morgonen och gå tills det
var ljust. Under stilleståndet fylldes vattenmagasinet. Detta
kraftverk betjänade byn ända tills 1934 då Hultafors Kraft blev
leverantör i Hedared. Detta medförde att bönderna efterhand
skaffade sig elektriska motorer och började gallra sina skogar.
Av detta virke tillverkades fisklådor för leverans till
Göteborg. Detta medförde ett stort uppsving för byn sista halvan
av 1930 talet. Priserna på lådorna var väldigt lågt, ca 65 öre i
Göteborg. Transporten kostade 10 öre per låda. En person sågade
och spikade 30 lådor/dag och högg i skogen till ca 100
lådor/dag. Spik till en låda kostade omkring 10 öre, tillkom
även elektrisk kraft. Det blev dock kontanter som kom in, det
var även nyttigt för skogen som därigenom blev gallrad.

.1

Gerd och hennes man Frank stannade kvar som anställda på
kontoret och Björn stannade också kvar ca 1 år till 1986, då han
köpte ett enbilsåkeri. Vid denna tid började konjunkturerna
vända uppåt igen och efterfrågan på betongvaror ökade.
Elementfabrikerna i Hestra och Hedared drevs nu även med ett
nattskift. Det visade sig vara helt rätt. Alternativet att bygga
ut fabrikerna hade varit en belastning då konjunkturerna vände
igen redan 1990.

Det finns en del i Sand & Betong som bara går uppåt. Det är
Kedddy spisar. Detta företag, igångvarande, köptes 1982 med
produktion av spisar, försäljningskontor i Kungsbacka och med
duktig personal som gick att återanställa. Spistillverkningen
överfördes till Hedared. Grundmaterialet är bims. Detta
importeras från Island och är ett vulkanskt slagg som tål höga
temperaturer. Materialet används även för skorstenselement som
tillverkas vid fabriken. Spisen som sådan tillverkas i byggdelar
och kan monteras upp av kunden på plats. När detta är gjort
påminner det om en tidigare "öppen spis". I eldstaden är det
plats för en gjutjärnskassett. Denna kassett gör att bränsle-
energin utnyttjas till 70%. Till skillnad från en öppen spis som
bara ger 5-10%. Det är många som köper gjutjärnskassetter för
inmurning i tidigare öppen spis. Detta är enormt effektivt. Om
spisen finns på lämpligt ställe i lägenheten håller den ensam
värmen med minimal vedåtgång. Dessa kassetter tillverkas på
metallgjuterier efter Sand & Betongs order och ritningar.

Hur ser Hedared ut idag?

Tidigt 70-tal byggdes det cirka 20 villor i Hedared beroende på
att Volvo anlade en testbana på Hällered. Testförarna önskade
bosätta sig i byn. Detta har blivit ett positivt inslag och de
flesta familjerna har blivit integrerade här. Det har även nu på
senare tillkommit ett 20-tal radhuslägenheter för uthyrning.
Detta är bra för byn. Som det nu blivit har äldre människor som
ej orkar sköta sin villa och trädgård sålt till nästa generation
och i stället hyrt lägenhet. Där kan livet förhoppningsvis
fortsätta några år då det går att leva mer på sparlåga under
lättare förhållande.

Vad det gäller vår idrottsförening så har fotbollen haft en
generationsväxling men är nu på väg upp igen. Bordtennisen står
sig enormt bra i konkurrensen. Med fina ledare och en enormt fin
ungdom som spelar. Föreningen har även byggt en bra klubbstuga.
Vi har även ett förstklassigt församlingshem nu i Hedared samt
nere vid fotbollsplanen finns även en bygdegård.

Jag tycker Hedared är ett litet men underbart ställe att fått
leva sitt liv i.

Hedared den 2 nov. 1993.

Göran

34

212

```
INGEMAR SAMUELSSON
MACHINIST, SAND & BETONG

TELEPHONE INTERVIEW, 04.22
```

Ingemar Samuelsson grew up in Hedared and has called it home for the entirety of his life, and like his father, has been a lifelong employee at Sand & Betong. Ingemar touched upon the importance of the factory, the notion of development and material knowledge passed down through generations.

Fadhel [00:09:32] Have you ever done basket making?

    Ingemar [00:09:33] No, I've never done it myself.

Fadhel [00:09:36] It's not your thing, so to speak?

    Ingemar [00:09:40] No... I've never taken a liking to it.

Fadhel [00:09:49] What has been your profession during your working life?

    Ingemar [00:09:51] I've worked with concrete in the industry.

Fadhel [00:09:58] At Sand & Betong?

    Ingemar [00:10:00] Yes, but they have a factory in Bollebygd, not far from Hedared. So I've been working there all these years.

Fadhel [00:10:06] What's the difference between the one in Hedared and the one in Bollebygd?

> **Ingemar [00:10:10]** Slightly different products, but everything ultimately ends up being made of concrete.

Fadhel [00:10:17] How come you started at Sand & Betong?

> **Ingemar [00:10:24]** Well, it's sort of like this: my father worked there, and when you finished school, you had to get a job, and it was the closest option at hand. This was in the 1980s when there was a bit of a financial crisis, so it was difficult for young people to find work. That's why I ended up in Bollebygd. I'm still employed, but I'm probably nearing the end now, so to speak.

Fadhel [00:11:03] Did you work alongside your father or other relatives?

> **Ingemar [00:11:12]** No, we've never worked together.

Fadhel [00:11:19] You mentioned the financial crisis, and the difficulty in finding a job. Thinking about how much Sand & Betong has meant for the village in terms of development, going from the cottage industry, with people making baskets, to the common man working at Sand & Betong... What do you think the opportunity for readily available employment has meant for the village?

> **Ingemar [00:11:48]** Well, it, of course, has meant quite a lot. It meant an upswing [in population and housing in the village], like when Volvo built their test tracks near Hedared, which made the village expand... There were two employers in Hedared: Sand & Betong, and Volvo Proving Ground. Between the two, it was where everyone worked, at least the men.

Fadhel [00:16:29] I've talked to Jan about the project to develop new housing in Hedared. The brochure they have made... What do you think about it?

Ingemar [00:16:40] I think it's great. I believe development is a must if the village is to survive.

Fadhel [00:16:51] You have to think differently, so to speak?

Ingemar [00:16:54] Yes, especially nowadays, you're not so dependent on local labour as before, because today you can commute differently. It's not so important that employees live in the village, but above all, things like the local supermarket in Hedared depend on its residents to keep operating: community life in general... There is a lot that requires people, simply put.

Fadhel [00:17:42] So development is important, to not be static, with the same 'setup' as before?

Ingemar [00:17:49] Yes, that's a common occurrence. If the village doesn't develop, it will almost be dismantled... It also depends on what kind of people move into the village, if they are driven individuals because that's what's needed to maintain businesses and community life.

Fadhel [00:18:30] What role do you think the Village Association plays regarding that? How important is the association in pushing for development in the village?

Ingemar [00:18:47] I think its [role] is important, there hasn't been anything else [to make new things happen]. Before, the Village Association was mostly involved in the 'older things' in the village: our history and the parish cottage etc.

Fadhel [00:19:02] To preserve?

Ingemar [00:19:06] Yes, to keep it alive. Today, some new people have come in [as part of the association], like Jan, in connection to their organisation, and suggestions that have come in [from the villagers] which have been listened to by the association, about new construction and developments etc.

Fadhel [00:20:11] So the idea of expansion came from the residents themselves?

Ingemar [00:20:18] Yes, I would say so, and then it was the Village Association who got that ball rolling.

...

Fadhel [00:25:19] So, industry is important, and it's also important with these voluntary associations, for maintaining the community feel in the village?

Ingemar [00:25:29] Yes, of course, one can't solely rely on and think it's the local municipality that should take care of our village. Something I came to think of when it comes to industry, in the village, basket making was quite common... But later, around the 1950s-60s, or at the beginning of the 1970s, people built what they called 'fishing boxes'. It was very common amongst the farmers and it was probably second to basket making.

Fadhel [00:26:35] Would you say it followed from basket making?

Ingemar [00:26:37] Yes. The men stood in the barn and made fishing boxes, buyers would then come and purchase them. My father did that. He made boxes and drove them to Gothenburg to be sold.

Fadhel [00:27:12] Did you ever help with the making?

Ingemar [00:27:22] No... I was too young. But we still have some boxes that he made, although they are now used for potatoes, with a little care they still work.

Fadhel [00:27:51] So we're thinking sometime in the 1950s-60s-70s? When did it start to fade away?

Ingemar [00:28:01] Yes... I would probably say it was in the 1970s when fewer and fewer people got into it for various reasons... It was then that many started working in the industry instead. No one wanted to do these jobs and began to go to Sand & Betong instead. The industry flourished, but the farms closed down.

Fadhel [00:28:47] Now that we have talked about basket making, fishing boxes, Sand & Betong etc... If we think about fifty years ahead, will we talk about Sand & Betong in the same way as we are talking about basket making now?

Ingemar [00:29:17] It's difficult to know really, hard to guess. If you think about Hedared's basket making like this: those who have moved to Hedared, have no idea, no clue, what the Hedared basket is, and might think it's a product made cheaply abroad. [The common knowledge] dies out in a way. But, as long as Sand & Betong are around, people will know it exists. If it were to be phased out, then maybe in twenty to thirty years, hardly anyone will know it existed, but then there's something else that takes over—that's how development works. Something else takes over. As long as Volvo is manufacturing their vehicles, which looks to continue for quite a long time to come, we will probably still be driving their cars... My children, who are around thirty years old, have a rough idea about what basket making is, but my grandchildren, in thirty years, probably won't know anything.

Fadhel [00:31:48] It takes two generations and then it fades out?

> **Ingemar [00:31:53]** I remember when Gustav was still making. I bought some of his baskets. I thought you needed to be quite manic to do such a thing, such work. He had different types of baskets, for different kinds of use, and developed them accordingly... The basket itself will still be there [in thirty years], absolutely, but the awareness and knowledge of it among common people will probably disappear.

```
IN-PERSON INTERVIEW
HEDARED, 09.22
```

Living on a family-inherited farm, Samuelsson still has some of the boxes made by his father in use. Although high in sentimental value, Ingemar mentioned their non-existing monetary value, as the wood they were made with was subpar. When meeting in Hedared, Samuelsson explained that sections of the buildings on his farm were constructed from salvaged wood, taken from older structures.

The practice of recycling 'good wood' from house to house was common in the past when quality materials were scarce and expensive.

Ingemar [00:05:07] People would move [closer to the village] from a log house nearer the forest, and then mark up the house and dismantle it. They might have had to cut the timber and adjust the logs a bit, but it was very common in the past, to partly dismantle or move an entire house, people had that knowledge.

Our home is also made with 'lying timber' which means we could [reuse it], we would only need to mark out the logs good enough to be moved... Way back when there was a relatively small amount of properly processed timber available, if you had access to this useful timber, then that type of material was worth its weight in gold, instead of having to take down a fir in the forest and process the tree from scratch. To be given already properly cut timber was a way to sustain.

...

Fadhel [00:33:15] I've asked everyone I've interviewed if there's an object, or a place in the area that symbolises Hedared for them. When you think of Hedared, what's the first thing that comes to mind?

Ingemar [00:33:48] What is the first thing I think of... Hedared is where I grew up. I don't know if there's ex- actly one place, it's the village. The entirety, you know. That's my security... I mean there's the stave church that's been there for [centuries]... But, for my own part, I just feel that Hedared [as a whole] is a familiar, and safe space to me.

Hedared kyrka, (Vestergötland.)

NOTES

1. Nationalencyklopedin (n.d.) *Bygd*.
    https://www.ne.se/uppslagsverk/ordbok/svensk/bygd [20/05/2024]. Translated by the author.
2. NE:s engelska ordbok (n.d.) *Hembygd*. https://www.ne.se/ordböcker [20/05/2024].
3. Nationalencyklopedin (n.d.) *Hembygd*.
    https://www.ne.se/uppslagsverk/encyklopedi/lång/hembygd [20/05/2024].
    Translated by the author.
4. 'Hembygdsrörelsen, a folk movement tasked with preserving, spreading knowledge about, and
    fostering an understanding of the culture of one's own hembygd, as well as safeguarding and
    maintaining its cultural heritage. Local hembygds associations and hembygds museums are
    primarily organised within hembygds federations or museum associations at county or provin-
    cial level.', NE Nationalencyklopedin. (2008) *NE i tre band: andra bandet*. Malmö: NE
    Nationalencyklopedin AB, p. 39. Translated by the author.
5. 'Hembygdsrörelsen in Sweden was established during the late 19th century and early 20th
    century. This period is often depicted as a turbulent time with significant societal transforma-
    tions, when interest in history and cultural heritage grew, influencing many different actors and
    areas of society.', Österberg, E. (1998) cited in Eskilsson, A. (2008) *På plats i historien: studier
    av hembygdsföreningar på 2000-talet*. Linköping: Linköpings universitet, pp. 9–10.
    Translated by the author.
6. 'The establishment of Hembygdsrörelsen in Sweden can thus be seen as part of a growing inter-
    est in cultural heritage in Sweden, but the trend was international. Björn-Ola Linnér describes
    the period 1880–1914 as the first major wave of preservation interest in the Western world, with
    various organisations seeking to preserve traces of a disappearing culture.', Linnér, B.O. (1998)
    cited in Eskilsson, A. (2008) *På plats i historien: studier av hembygdsföreningar på 2000-talet*.
    Linköping: Linköpings universitet, p. 10. Translated by the author.

    To further contextualise the period during which Hembygdsrörelsen emerged:

    6.1. 'Interest in folk culture grew significantly during the late 19th and early 20th
          centuries. Newspapers were filled with depictions of rural life, and local heritage
          associations sprang up like mushrooms. Folk culture was at the height of fashion.
          At the same time, a more institutionalised and systematic exploration of folk tradi-
          tions emerged. The Swedish Parliament took on an increasing responsibility for
          documenting intangible cultural heritage, and government funds were allocated to
          the study of folk traditions.', Skotte, F. (2008) *Folkets Minnen: Traditionsinsamling
          i idé och praktik 1919–1964*. Göteborg: The Institute for Language and Folklore and
          Göteborgs universitet, p. 14. Translated by the author.
    6.2. 'The upper class already had its history, but those who lie forgotten in the common
          ground of the churchyard have none. And yet, it was they who built Sweden.
          Now, their lives shall be brought to light, their culture made known.',
          Jansson (2005), quoted in Skotte, F. (2008) *Folkets Minnen: Traditionsinsamling i idé
          och praktik 1919–1964*. Göteborg: The Institute for Language and Folklore and
          Göteborgs universitet, p. 100. Translated by the author.

7. Sveriges Hembygdsförbund (2023) *About the Swedish Local Heritage Federation*.
    https://www.hembygd.se/shf/about-the-swedish-local-heritage-federation-1 [2024-06-10]
8. Ibid.
9. Sveriges Hembygdsförbund (2024) *Det här är hembygd*.
    https://www.hembygd.se/shf/det-har-ar-hembygd-1 [2024-06-10]. Translated by the author.
10. Hela Sverige ska leva (n.d.) *Rural Sweden*.
    https://www.helasverige.se/om-oss/rural-sweden/ [2024-06-10].
11. Ibid.
12. Ibid.
13. Hela Sverige ska leva (n.d.) *Hur arbetar vi i Hela Sverige ska leva Sjuhärad*.
    https://www.helasverige.se/sjuharad/var-verksamhet/ [2024-06-10]. Translated by the author.

IMAGE CREDITS

Unless specified, all images were either taken by the author in 2022, sourced from the author's personal photo albums or found in the parish cottage in Hedared. In the latter cases, the dates and the photographer's identity are unknown.

p. 150:
Aerial image of Hedared (1951). Photo: AB Flygtrafik/Vänersborgs museum.
p. 152:
Aerial image of Hedared (1959–1961). Photo: Lantmäteriet.
p. 154:
In Thoughts, *Together* (2023). Photo: Alexis Rodríguez Cancino.

LOOKING BACK
TO GO FORWARD

TANYA HARROD

IN THE EARLY TWENTIETH CENTURY part of being modern was to be anti-modern. There was, as the social historian Jose Harris observed, 'a lurking grief at the memory of a lost domain—a sense that change was inevitable, in many respects desirable, but that its gains were being purchased at a terrible price'.[1] Harris was writing about Edwardian Britain but the sense of loss was Europe-wide. The German poet Rainer Maria Rilke observed in 1925: 'Even for our grandparents, a 'House', a 'Well', a familiar tower, their very dress, their cloak, was infinitely more intimate: almost everything a receptacle in which they both found and enlarged a store of humanness... The animated, experienced things that share our lives are running out, and cannot be replaced. We are perhaps the last to have known such things'.[2]

This fear of erasure of familiar materials, environments and techniques floats up in the Cambridge literary critic F.R. Leavis's writings about a lost 'organic community'.[3] The text that most inspired Leavis was George Sturt's classic *The Wheelwright's Shop*, published in 1923. Sturt had inherited the two-century old wheelwrighting business from his father. As an educated man he felt an outsider, but as an outsider he set out to describe the indescribable—the tacit skills involved in building horse-drawn waggons and waggon wheels. His task was difficult because his employees' knowledge was, as Sturt explained, 'set out in no book. It was not scientific. I never met a man who professed any other than an empirical acquaintance with the waggon-builder's lore... The lore was a tangled network of country prejudices, whose reasons were known in some respects here, in others there, and so on. ...for the most part the details were but dimly understood; the whole body of knowledge was a mystery, a piece of folk knowledge, residing in the folk collectively, but never wholly in any individual'.[4]

Sturt was attempting to articulate a deep understanding of a specific material. He was setting out to describe what Michael Baxandall, in the context of the limewood sculptors of Germany, called the 'chiromancy' of wood.[5] Sturt explained that farm waggons were made of tough slender pieces of wood 'with just the right curve'. These were natural curves, not steam bent, and the wheelwrights selected their material from wood-lands that they knew intimately. Indeed, everything was done on an intimate scale. By the 1920s Sturt's wheelwright's shop, which he had inherited in 1884, had become a motor repair shop. Any attempt to go against this apparently inevitable flow would be, Sturt reflected, small-scale. The recuperation of cen-turies of woodcraft knowledge would inevitably be limited. Timber, Sturt wrote, had turned into 'a sort of enslaved and hu-miliating padding for steel'.[6]

The design processes described by Sturt were highly flexible, a characteristic that came to fascinate members of the 'Design Methods' movement in the 1960s and 1970s. Inspired by the vernacular trial-and-error methodology recorded by Sturt, figures like the visionary design theorist John Chris Jones argued in favour of interdisciplinary teamwork as against the individual designer working with a drawing board, remote from craft and process.[7] Jones was describing a world where the drawing board was the designer and architect's tool. Now large-ly replaced by some kind of 3D software, the problems remain the same as when Jones wrote of the pencil-wielding designer: 'It's just a grotesque procrustean exercise. It's bound to seem very satisfactory to the designers because they see this beau-tiful bird's eye view and they can control it...it's bound to seem an imposition to the users. But the users will not be aware it's miles from what they want, they'll be tricked into accepting the professional values'.[8] Waggons may have been swept away by the motorised vehicle, but Jones felt they were worth our atten-tion as objects within a culture because of the close relations between makers and users. John Chris Jones was not the only designer in the mid- to late-twentieth century to recognise that the long evolution which created perfect waggons was a collec-tive process quite different to the work of the modern designer.

In Italy, eminent architects and designers also turned to vernacular cultures as a model for new ways of living. They looked back to go forward. Research was aided by the contin-uance of pre-industrial ways of life in Italy. As the architect Alessandro Poli wrote of peasant culture: 'There is an enor-mous heritage of knowledge to be found in this subordinate, marginal society, in which we can trace not only the roots of our science but also the possibility of a different science, an alternative way of living and planning'. In 1974 Poli took as his guide Zeno, a peasant from Tuscany, who built everything he needed with his own hands, each object dictated by necessity alone. To Poli's eyes these things, many connected to viticulture, were 'loaded with expressive richness'.[9]

Meanwhile another Italian designer, Enzo Mari, sought ways in which agency could be returned to individuals. In 1974 Mari circulated plans for simple self-build furniture—his 'Proposta per un'autoprogettazione'. In 1973 Mari had tried, and failed, to unleash creativity in a porcelain factory by creating a cast porcelain kit of parts which workers could assemble as they saw fit. And in 1989 he held an exhibition of sixty-six scythes at the Galleria Danese in Milan. 'Perché una mostra di falci?'

Perché indeed.

Mari was wanting to learn from the vernacular in the same way as Sturt, Jones and Poli. A properly functioning scythe answered a primary need. As a product still used widely in the third world it had to be cheap, it had to be highly efficient and it had to be capable of being maintained by the owner. Mari observed that scythes were still being made in Italy using 'artisan wisdom', based on 5,000 years of 'constant refinement and revision', and while Mari was not dreaming of a 'mythic primitivism'—agriculture in Europe was highly mechanised—he believed that there was much to be learned from the scythe and its high quality, its functionality and low cost.[10]

Waggons, a Tuscan peasant's sieve for viticulture, self-build furniture, and scythes can be seen as marginal objects, albeit pregnant with meaning. One activity, weaving, has a continuity that defies the depredations and progressions of modernity. Weavers, whether designing for industry or working as artists, necessarily look back in order to look forward, studying the distant present of peasant or vernacular weaving from remoter parts of Europe, or investigating ancient Egyptian linens or pre-Columbian Andean textiles, the latter recognised as being technically among the greatest weavings ever created. The act of weaving has never unravelled—even if we may deplore so-called 'tapestries' made from designs by contemporary artists on computerised jacquard looms, and lament the generalised lack of interest in the poetics of weaving technology.

I like to think of basketry as a branch of weaving, a form of weaving without a loom, and if made of natural materials, resistant to standardisation. Fadhel Mourali, whose research this publication celebrates, is the great-grandson of a man known as 'the last basket maker from Risa'. Mourali's research investigates that claim and honours his ancestor's memory. But Mourali also belongs to an all-encompassing tradition that will never record a 'last maker'. Weaving has always transcended gender and national boundaries and it is arguably the world's oldest technology, intrinsic to myth and to legend, rooted in the beginnings of human interaction, touchingly close to one of the world's most beautiful activities, the building of nests by birds. As we have seen, some kinds of collective knowledge are fragile.

Scythes are still manufactured in Europe but wheel-wrighting and waggon making now exist only in a limited museological fashion. Meanwhile in Nigeria hand-built low-fired functional pots for open fire cooking and water cooling are still speedily made by extraordinarily skilled women. To watch a Gwari woman make such a pot is one of the world's wonders. But this is a craft, art and technology that depends on whole communities of committed makers and, just as important, users. Cookers and fridges have already undermined this remarkable niche technology, just as tractors and trucks undermined the wheelwright's trade. And only forty years ago I came across a group of Welsh farmers scything a field. In that remote place in Gwynedd it is conceivable that they scythe still on steep and uneven ground. By contrast, Mourali's weaving—and all weaving—is part of an elemental global interconnected activity that will surely always be with us. I like to think weaving techniques in all their multifarious variousness will never be entirely lost, and will always be reviewed afresh, over and over.

The passing of weaving would draw a line under the survival of humanity.

Therein lies its fascination and its immemorial power, going back to look forward.

Dr Tanya Harrod is the author of the prize-winning The Crafts in Britain in the Twentieth Century (Yale University Press 1999). She contributes regularly to The Burlington Magazine, The Guardian, Crafts and the Literary Review. She is on the Advisory Panel of The Burlington Magazine and is Advisor to the Craft Lives Project based at the National Sound Archive of the British Library. She is a member of the International Association of Art Critics, of the London-based Critic's Circle and an Honorary Brother of the Art Workers Guild. With Glenn Adamson and Edward S. Cooke she is the co-founder of The Journal of Modern Craft. The Last Sane Man: Michael Cardew, modern pots, colonialism and the counterculture (Yale University Press, 2012) won the 2012 James Tait Black Prize for biography. Her most recent books are The Real Thing: essays on making in the modern world (Hyphen Press, 2015), Leonard Rosoman (Royal Academy, 2016), Craft, Whitechapel Gallery 2018 (part of the series Documents of Contemporary Art) and Humankind: Ruskin Spear, class, culture and art in 20th century Britain, Thames & Hudson and Francis Bacon Estate 2022. She is currently working on a double life of the brother and sister Rolf and Margaret Gardiner.

NOTES

1. Jose Harris, *Private Lives, Public Spirit: Britain 1870–1914*, (1993) London: Penguin Books, 1994, p. 36.
2. J. Leischman, *Rilke: New Poems*, New York: New Directions, 1964, p. 17.
3. See F.R. Leavis, Denys Thompson, *Culture and Environment: The Training of Critical Awareness*, London: Chatto & Windus, 1933.
4. George Sturt, *The Wheelwright's Shop*, Cambridge: CUP, 1923, pp. 73–74.
5. Michael Baxandall, *The Limewood Carvers of Renaissance Germany*, London & New Haven: Yale University Press, 1980, pp. 32–38.
6. George Sturt, *The Wheelwright's Shop*, Cambridge: CUP, 1923, p. 74.
7. C. Thomas Mitchell, *Redefining Designing: From Form to Experience*, New York: Van Nostrand Reinhold, 1993, pp. 38–60.
8. C. Thomas Mitchell, ibid., p. 42.
9. Alessandro Poli, 'Nearing the Moon to Earth', in *Other Space Odysseys*, eds. Giovanna Borasi and Mirko Zardini, Montreal: Canadian Centre for Architecture/Baden: Lars Müller Publishers, 2010, pp. 112–115.
10. See Hans Ulrich Obrist with Francesca Giacomelli, *Enzo Mari*, Milano: La Triennale & Electa S.p.A, 2020, pp. 165–166.

DESIGNING THROUGH SLÖJD

HELENA HANSSON

FROM MY PERSPECTIVE, craftsmanship is a way of life. Craft is about the art of taking control over one's life.

In parts of this text, the Swedish word for craft and craftsmanship, *slöjd*,[1] will be used. The word slöjd derives from the old Nordic words *slögher* and *slöghth* meaning cunning, knowledgeable, and handy, which represent craftsmanship and artistry.[2] Individuals who practice slöjd will therefore be referred to as *slöjdare*, meaning craftsmen.

To me, a slöjdare is a person who quite literally takes matters into their own hands, using their cunning, knowledge and sleight to solve an emerging problem with what is at hand. It should be noted that I am not a slöjdare myself, but, in my capacity as a design researcher and lecturer, I understand what slöjd, and its practitioners, can achieve. In short, I design through slöjd. In my practice, I invite slöjdare into my design process. Their presence contributes to shaping the choices made for the overall making process. It is a collaborative effort and a mode of practice that I try to further explore and apply in my day-to-day work as a lecturer at HDK-Valand – Academy of Art and Design, University of Gothenburg.

I believe that the more complex and abstract a design issue is, the more we need a bodily experience to comprehend the change that is happening.[3] I, therefore, emphasise 'the slöjd approach' in my teaching: a return to the origins of design, which has traditionally been deeply rooted in a material culture.[4] The idea of adapting a slöjd approach in my work as a teacher and design researcher started during my doctoral studies (which took place between 2012–2021). Building upon the belief that slöjd is about taking control over one's life, formed a basis for further exploration throughout my PhD. During field studies in Kisumu, in the western part of Kenya, I collaborated with local basket makers to understand the terms under which they were practising their slöjd. I observed how the local slöjdare, the Jua Kali, were experts in making use of the things they had around them. Locally grown materials, or even waste materials, were by simple means transformed into desirable objects. I realised we have much to learn from one another.

In this context, I as a designer had to be frugal and adapt to the local conditions to be able to design sustainably.

This is when I started to design *through* slöjd.

Such art, of making use of what you have around you, was in Kenya, a survival strategy. The resource scarcity, insufficient governmental support structures, and lack of formal job opportunities created affordability constraints, i.e. the financial means available did not allow craftspeople to buy more than they needed. These frugal conditions forced people to become creative and innovative, which is what I refer to as frugal design in my thesis. In a broader environmental context, I consider adopting a frugal design approach (making use of what is around us) as crucial to implement the necessary changes and achieve the sustainability goals outlined in the UN Agenda 2030, in short; 'to do more with less'.[5]

Today, I try to embrace the frugal approach even if I am located in another part of the globe, with other local and socio-economic conditions. I have started the platform Designing Together which focuses on the collaborative aspects of making, and adapting to a frugal design approach. I am engaged in two research projects, Transforming the City for Play, and Hephaestus, collaborating with slöjdare Karl Hallberg as one of my closest research partners. He belongs to the artist-led cooperative Not Quite in rural Fengersfors, Sweden. At Not Quite, Hallberg (and other slöjdare) excel in the art of utilisation: being knowledgeable and using their sleight to solve a problem with what is at hand, a person which the French social anthropologist Claude Lévi-Strauss would call a *bricoleur*.

In his book *The Savage Mind* (1966), Lévi-Strauss writes how the artist as a bricoleur 'shapes the beautiful and useful out of the dump heap of human life'.[6] Lévi-Strauss compared this artistic production process to that of a handyman, who solves technical or mechanical problems with any materials, a kind of 'jack-of-all-trades'. The word *bricolage* is a French loanword meaning 'the process of improvisation in a human endeavour'. The name originates from the French verb *bricoler* ('to tinker'), with the English term D-I-Y ('Do-It-Yourself') being the nearest equivalent to the modern French usage. In both languages, bricolage also denotes the works or products that originate from do-it-yourself endeavours.[7]

In art, bricolage is seen as a technique or a creative approach. Works are constructed from various available materials, which often characterise a postmodern art practice. Bricolage can also be seen as a kind of curatorial practice, as it remixes, reconstructs, and reuses separate materials or artefacts to thereby create new meanings and insights.[8] These are the characteristics that form the central role of slöjd in my design process, which manifests as a kind of slöjd-bricolage. I use this concept in my teaching and try to train my students in understanding that design is not a one-man show, but rather a *D-I-T* ('Do-It-Together') activity.

As the design process involves many actors, I call such a collective veil activity for *sam-slöjd*, 'co-craft'. The term was coined in 2013 by Professor Otto von Busch,[9] researcher and lecturer at Parsons School of Design in New York, another of my closest research partners. The prototype for our future collaborations was a workshop for professional slöjdare at Sätergläntan Institute of Crafts in Sweden. With a care for the surrounding materials, we 'hacked' the local train station using a slöjd-approach: we remodelled benches at the local train station, extending them to make room for more commuters, and allow for the possibility of more interpersonal interactions. As written in our latest article, von Busch and I define the term co-craft as a 'collaborative mode of crafts, where participants not only work together but become reliant on each other'.[10] Following the ideas of craftsmaker and thinker William Coperthwaite, such collaborative design tools 'make democratic ideals tangible',[11] which we refer to as socially valid designs.[12]

Together with von Busch and Hallberg, I have in recent years explored what socially valid design is within a co-crafting context. In both a practical and theoretical sense, we have striven to understand what co-craft, within our current forms of collaboration, can do, and what it possibly could achieve. In our case, an example of socially valid design is when Hallberg created a new tool consisting of two saws welded together at the front. The double saw was used in design activities which had a focus on youth engagement.

The new tool was designed to make the workload not only more efficient but increase the degree of cooperation between participants. When learning to use the tool the participants were made reliant on each other, turning the making process into a trust-building exercise. The double saw manifested that you are stronger when working together, but also emphasised that collaboration requires training in specific skills, for the participant to be empathetic, and be in constant conversation with the other co-crafter.

Engaging in co-craft activities forms a development continuum: learning to master local materials and techniques during the interaction with others. Participation in this kind of activity provides new skills and an understanding of the knowledge held in one's hands. This new understanding empowers the participant to comprehend their own ability, and connection to others, to their immediate surroundings or to the planet at large. The participant gains independence and power over their own life, which in turn fosters change to become tangible and concrete. Enabled to take matters into their own hands, and use their knowledge to solve an emerging problem with what is *at* hand.

Practising what (for me) is the essence of slöjd.

In times of division and uncertainty, we as people are becoming increasingly separated from one another. I believe slöjd reconnects us to a collective understanding of what unites us. It links past and present, local and global, and reminds us of the inherent relationship between humans and nature. It embodies empowerment, trust-building and serves an important role as a 'weaving element', when uniting these components.

For these reasons, I propose that we as designers need to act more as slöjdare and bricoleurs, whose role is to act as agents for change, that are concretising ideas of change in a tangible reality, together with others—continuing to practise and assemble new forms of socially valid design.

Helena Hansson is a lecturer at HDK-Valand — Academy of Art and Design, University of Gothenburg, Sweden, where she also holds a Ph.D. in design. She has a background in design, transdisciplinary research and craft, and in her doctoral thesis, she explored participatory design in a Global North-South cooperation context (Sweden and Kenya). She is particularly interested in collaborative and community-building processes, focusing on practice-based methodologies for craft and frugal design.

NOTES

1. 'The Swedish word *Slöjd* has been retained with its proper orthography; there is no good reason apparent why an attempt should either be made to translate it, or to write for it its phonetic equivalent. It has, by this time, surely acquired the right to be considered a proper lexicographical element of English; the more so, as there is no single word in the language to express the idea it unmistakably conveys. It is only necessary to bear in mind, once for all, that in its pronunciation *öj* is practically equivalent to the English *oi*.', Carpenter, W. H., quoted in Salomon, O. (1888) *The Slöjd in the Service of the School*. Translated by W. H. Carpenter. New York: Industrial Education Association, preface.

2. Hartman, S., (Ed.), (2014) *Slöjd, bildning och kultur*. Stockholm: Carlsson Bokförlag.

3. Like Professor Otto von Busch[3.1] at Parsons School of Design in New York, I claim that the more complex and abstract a design issue is, the more we need a bodily experience to comprehend the change that is happening. I primarily teach on the MFA Embedded Design programme which enables students to unlock the role of design within diverse organisational contexts and meet growing demands for sustainable, innovative, and disruptive design. During my twenty years of teaching as a university lecturer, I have noticed an increased abstraction and theorisation in academia. Complex design issues, such as the ones highlighted in Agenda 2030 (the UN's sustainability goals) are often dealt with on a 'meta-level'.[3.2] Modern-day design students are trained to map and visualise complexities and critically discuss change potentialities instead of dealing with the actual change in a 'tangible reality'.[3.3]

    3.1 von Busch, O. (2022) *Making Trouble: Design and Material Activism*. London: Bloomsbury Publishing.

    3.2 Ibid.

    3.3 Sennett, R. (2008). *The Craftsman*. London: Arrow Book.

4. Koskinen, I., Zimmerman, J., Binder, T., Redström, J., Wensveen, S. (2011) 'Building Research Programs'. In: Roumeliotis, R., Bevans, D. (Eds.), *Design Research Through Practice: From the Lab, Field, and Showroom*. Waltham: Elsevier, pp. 175–176.

5. Woolridge, 2010; Bhatti and Ventresca, 2013; Radjou and Prabhu, 2015; Leadbeater, 2014; Pesa, 2015; Lillo, 2020; Hansson, 2021.

6. Lévi-Strauss, C. (1962) *La Pensée Sauvage*. Paris. English translation as *The Savage Mind* (1966). Chicago, Illinois: University of Chicago Press, p. 33.

7. Baldick, C. (2008) *The Oxford Dictionary of Literary Terms*. Oxford; New York: Oxford University Press, p. 42. Broady, E. (2005) *Colloquial French 2: The Next Step in Language Learning*. New York: Routledge, p. 77.

8. Moon Hyland, C. (2011) *Materials and Media in Art Therapy: Critical Understandings of Diverse Artistic Vocabularies*. Oxon: Routledge, p. 99.

9. von Busch, O. (2013) 'Collaborative Craft Capabilities: The Bodyhood of Shared Skills'. In: *The Journal of Modern Craft*, Volume 6, 2013—Issue 2, pp. 135–146.

10. Hansson, H and von Busch, O. (2023) 'Socially valid tools: Sloydtrukk and co-crafting togetherness.' In: *Craft Research*, Volume 14, 2023—Issue 1, pp. 59–79.

11. Coperthwaite, W. and Saltmarsh J. (2007) *A Handmade Life: In Search of Simplicity*. White River Junction, Vermont: Chelsea Green Publishing Company.

12. Hansson, H and von Busch, O. (2023) 'Socially valid tools: Sloydtrukk and co-crafting togetherness.' In: *Craft Research*, Volume 14, 2023—Issue 1, p. 59.

DEFINITIONS OF SLÖJD

PART OF THE INITIAL SHOWCASE of this project included a panel at the Textile Museum of Sweden. The panel aimed to expand the conversation surrounding the project's focal points, to delve deeper into the interplay between the principles of traditional slöjd processes and their expressions in art and design. The Textile Museum is located in my hometown of Borås, in the heart of the Seven Districts, and is housed within the walls of an old textile factory. It shares the building (now named Fashion Textile Center) with the Swedish School of Textiles and other cultural and educational institutions.

The Textile Museum, like its sister-institution Borås Museum of History, has a rich archive, primarily focused on documenting the former textile production that took place in the region. The museum emerged in response to the local textile industry's decline in the second half of the twentieth century. Its operations stand to safeguard the remnants of a bygone era, not only through an extensive collection, but through its ongoing programme of exhibitions and events. Today, the museum showcases contemporary textile excellence on an international scale, while continuing to nurture the rich textile heritage of Sjuhärad.

The permanent exhibition *Textil Kraft* (Textile Power) exemplifies this, it illustrates the transformation of small-scale rural production becoming industrious production lines in factories belonging to local companies such as Svenskt Konstsilke (whose former factory the museum now resides in). From a Sjuhärad perspective, visitors are guided through a textile production and garment manufacturing journey, from its local historical roots to its current global position.

The exhibit showcases this evolution by displaying various types of machinery used in procurement processes and sheds light on the communities who have been, and continue to be, the makers of the end products.

What better place to anchor a conversation about the evolution of craft?

Slöjd — 'Craft'
Slöjdare — 'Craftsman' / 'Craftsperson'
Slöjda — 'To Craft'

Under the banner: *To be and to become: identity in slöjd, art and design—in and out of the Seven Districts*, I opened the discussion to present the project, its objectives, and my initial findings in all their layers. One of the invited speakers was Sara Degerfält. Degerfält works as a *Hemslöjdskonsulent*, a Handicraft Advisor, at the Cultural Administration in the Västra Götaland region.

When asked to present her relationship to craft, Sara described an experience she had at the age of twenty-one, when participating in an international youth exchange programme in a village located in North-East Thailand. The village was active in cotton and silk production, with fibres grown for the traditional Ikat weaving technique. Degerfält described seeing the villagers having such a strong understanding of, and deep connection to, their land, and the conditions needed to enable the procurement of textile materials.

The experience stayed with her.

Degerfält wanted to learn what the Swedish equivalent was—to understand the natural conditions needed for material procurement in Sweden. She enrolled as a weaving student at Sätergläntan Institute of Crafts, an epicentre for traditional crafts in north Sweden. Here, Degerfält was taught how to process wool and linen: cultivate, spin, and ultimately weave these fibres. As a handicraft advisor, Degerfält's role is to enable public engagement with traditional craft practices and to promote an understanding of how raw materials can become everyday items through doing-it-yourself.

Sara described her time at Sätergläntan, and the entire Swedish 'hemslöjds movement',[1] as being built upon a reverence for the *allmoge* tradition.[2] Degerfält expressed her affection for its aesthetics. More specifically, her intrigue with allmoge comes from a sort of meta-perspective—what is the overarching fascination of slöjdare with the allmoge tradition? Why did embroidery motifs from earlier eras, crafted in

240

specific stitches, experience a resurgence in popularity during the 1950s and 60s? Furthermore, Degerfält explained that her creative process frequently involves a recreation of tradition through material and technique.

***

I have come to understand that trying to define slöjd is an age-old task. When revisiting heritage and tradition through this project, I have been reintroduced to slöjd and its many nuances, resulting in a greater understanding of slöjd in all its facets. Before embarking on this project, my only encounter with slöjd was limited to my school days, within the four walls of a classroom.[3] The slöjd curriculum encompassed woodwork and textiles (with a focus on sewing, knitting, and crocheting). Attendance was mandatory, as with any other class, and upon completing a set number of tasks, students had the liberty to select their preferred avenue: wood or textiles. Material-specific terms of slöjd exist depending on the medium, hence why the classes were referred to as wood-slöjd or textile-slöjd. Naturally, I gravitated towards the latter.

At the time, I likened the class to any other laborious subject—compulsory and mundane. There were criteria to be met and objects to be made. Nothing more, nothing less.

I had never thought of (or experienced) slöjd as a potential gateway to something greater—a medium for self-expression or a skill that could become a profession. To me, slöjd was presented as a strict 'thing' with clear rules of what was right and what was most certainly wrong. It was not an avenue for personal expression. Its mission sought uniformity and repetition, and within that space, I felt confined.

So, at the moment of our panel at the Textile Museum, having been reintroduced to slöjd through this project, and fascinated by all its potential, I was keen to get a first-hand understanding of Sara Degerfält's view on slöjd. The following transcript is taken from our discussion, highlighting the dialogue between Degerfält and me when exploring some of the distinctive characteristics of slöjd.

Fadhel [00:15:29]: The word slöjd. It originates from the old word 'slöghþ' which can be translated to diligence, wisdom, being skillful and inventive. To engage with slöjd means to, with the help of various tools, transform a material into an object, like the Hedared basket.

The perseverance that exists in slöjd, to be able to build something from scratch, to understand a material and a method... As a handicraft advisor, what can be gained from slöjd?

Sara [00:15:59]: I studied several years at university, and have worked with this professionally for seven years, and I still struggle with the definition of slöjd, and I also think that is the beauty of it. The term slöjd has as many definitions as there are practitioners. But if we had to connect slöjd to a set of values: [which Sara refers to as being the modern thing to do], function, technique, and material come on top of the list of 'core values' that slöjd embodies, which differentiates slöjd from other things, like art. In slöjd, function and material even go above aesthetics at times, which signifies it even more.

Fadhel [00:17:03]: Is it the longing or reverence for tradition that makes things like function take precedence over aesthetics?

Sara [00:17:18]: Well, one idea that is prominent in slöjd is: 'I take what I have, and I do what I should'. The material often gets to take the lead, guiding the outcome, which in turn becomes defined by the material, of course, these processes are guided by your technical ability and prior knowledge of the material.

Fadhel [00:17:53]: So it is guided by a set of rules? In having prior knowledge to understand how to navigate [the material]?

Sara [00:18:01]: Slöjd is to have this deep knowledge. I want to do something, and then it's the *how*. If I put on more twist [when spinning a yarn], there's no right or wrong, there are only different results, and that you comprehend what is happening, with each result. So if you apply more twist to a yarn, then it becomes stronger, and maybe that's your end goal, and when you weave, that, in turn, makes [the cloth] more water-proof, but if you twist it too much, it'll break. That knowledge is something you need to have in your hands, and that, that is slöjd.

Again, going back to the idea of 'core values', in today's society we speak a lot about sustainability, and I think sustainability is something that has been mentioned within the slöjd movement since the Inland ice went away, and people started to populate our lands. That is how long the conversation about sustainability has been around in a slöjd context. The whole point of making things is so that they sustain, that they are durable and don't break, and if they do break, then you should be able to fix them. That is sustainability.

Fadhel [00:19:12]: *Att slöjda* ('to craft') often means reconstructing tradition with your skills—looking back to be able to look forward through one's making.

Is it somehow possible to decipher the present through a slöjd process?

243

Sara [00:19:30]: First and foremost, to be able to understand the variables of twisting a yarn and understanding [the construction] of your everyday items is a question of power. If you don't know how clothes work, if you can't fix them, you will, per definition, be a bit of a poorer person because of it, and I think that is what makes slöjd so incredibly important.

If you think about the present, the term 'historyless' comes to mind, a concept you can fill with many different things. One aspect is that one doesn't regard history as important, that having historical knowledge is not important for things in the future or in the now, and I think we all can agree that's something bad. But then, a great question is: what can you do to not lack historical awareness? Well, one solution would be to learn about history. One way of doing this is to read a book about a man who walked across an ice,[4] who happened to be a king or reconstruct the whole costume worn by the Bocksten Man,[5] which takes a very long time. Then, you understand history, not by residing years, but through your hands, and that connects you to a person who did the same thing seven hundred years ago. That is super cool.

I have this short story written in my head, titled 'What the Bocksten man has taught me about our current times'. The Bocksten man lived in a very different period than we, say what you will about the 1300s, with raging wars everywhere, but Earth Overshoot Day[6] wasn't in [August] like it is now. These are things I can't stop thinking about.

When working with the Bocksten man's clothing, I realised that his shirt was made with an incredibly small piece of cloth. Even with such a small amount of material, you were still able to make a three-dimensional garment with this tiny two-dimensional piece of fabric.

244

It would have been super expensive, but people still had the knowledge and resourcefulness. Today, we might call that 'zero waste making', so we have an incredible amount to learn, looking back.

Fadhel [00:22:35]: So you learn with your hands, speaking with yourself as you're making, instead of just reading about it in a book?

Sara [00:22:46]: I am in conversation with the object. If I want to recreate a pair of socks, the Bocksten man's costume, or something else, I start a conversation with the item at hand, then let yesteryear tell me things, and I listen. Something that is also significant in slöjd, and again, contrary to art, is that you are allowed to mimic others. This is another component, part of the core values of slöjd, and its tradition; we can take all this knowledge, the trials and errors of others before us, and then we put all those things together, and we create something new that builds on what others before us have done. I can become just as good, in the best case, maybe even better, or worse, because it is not certain that I am better at something than the one making it in the past. But you have the freedom to borrow, which I think is great.

Fadhel [00:23:47]: Freely sharing knowledge... So there's an openness that infiltrates slöjd?

Sara [00:23:53]: It is made/built on a kind of 'adding on', that is a huge building block of the essence of slöjd, as I see it.

***

[In relation to my own work, making a filament yarn consisting of biodegradable PLA plastic and the remains of wood fibres from the making of Hedared baskets, I was curious to know what Sara, in her capacity as a handicraft advisor, thought of these elements.]

***

Fadhel [00:34:34]: What do you think of 'new' materials making their way into tradition?

> Sara [00:34:41]: I think we're back at the point where slöjd becomes something undefinable. Before, the role of the handicraft advisor was to make sure rag rugs were beaten thoroughly enough when weaving to produce an accurate result—we don't do that anymore. We say no to all those requests. The way I see it, we are not the ones that define slöjd, we are the ones that listen, that is our role, and if someone comes and says: 'I want to make Hedared baskets, and I am going to use biodegradable plastic together with its pine fibre and 3D print it', then I just say: 'OK. Great!' My job is not to think something is good or bad, or to have an opinion, it is to follow and observe what is happening at the moment.

Fadhel [00:36:14]: Going back to the openness in slöjd as a core value... Why is it important to interpret slöjd from new perspectives?

> Sara [00:36:26]: Good question, now I started to continue reflecting on your last question. I often work with our 'hemslöjds heritage', its thoughts and approaches, which came to be at a point in time, at a sort of crossroads: the hemslöjds movement was used to counteract industrialism. This is when a few of these core values of slöjd were established: the work of the hand in contrast to the machine. And I think that's why you just asked this question before, because what happens when you take this extremely craft-based technique and put it into an industrial process? I just needed to share that. What was your new question?

Fadhel [00:37:20]: Why is it important to interpret slöjd from new perspectives?

Sara [00:37:24]: Well, I think maybe that's just it. Whatever happens, happens. The way people *slöjdar* ('craft') today is a product of our present, and you need to follow along that process.

Fadhel [00:37:42]: To let it be in motion?

Sara [00:37:45]: Yes. As handicraft advisors, we can contribute and support with different perspectives through initiatives, but to decide and define, that is not something that I do, at least. I mean, new perspectives and new generations are constantly coming forward, and everyone needs to have the space to do their own thing. If we don't allow room for that, then there is no room for progression or development, and everything we have will just halt, and remain history.

Fadhel [00:38:18]: So [slöjd] has to be in motion, and non-static?

Sara [00:38:21]: Yes exactly, you cannot think of slöjd or anything for that matter as static, because then you lose it.

In the early stages of this project, Sara Degerfält introduced me to Helena Hansson and her research. This led me to discover how theory can intersect with practice—how theory can inform slöjd, and vice versa.

During my undergrad, the general curriculum was primarily focused on hands-on making. I was taught how to practise textile design by developing compositions of colour and texture. Although this was the purpose of the course: to master the making of textiles through visually harmonious compositions; questions of the greater social, cultural, or environmental realities of practising textiles were (for me) often left overlooked in favour of the purely visual. In light of this, Hansson's research demonstrated a more purposeful role for the designer. It offered a pathway for me to engage with the much sought-after deeper layers of meaning attached to the design process. Her work and its engagement with slöjd *and* theoretical concepts broadened my perspective on how to more purposefully articulate and approach my research related to the basket.

Naturally, Hansson was one of the first people I interviewed for my dissertation. During our conversation, Helena explained that her research focused on developing and building on existing knowledge structures rather than aiming to create something completely new, where collaborative efforts between design and slöjd together address social, economic, or environmental challenges. In the context of her research, Hansson described the role of a designer as akin to a weaver—a 'connector' of various types of knowledge—moving between actors, practice and research: collaborative partners, practical making, and abstract theory. Hansson explained that the designer often becomes a centralised, authoritative and 'prince-like' figure in a design process. She argued that designers need to act more as a decentralising force within a collaboration; like a spider weaving a web, designers should be in constant motion, curious and open to exploring new concepts, perspectives and connections.

By adopting this exploratory mode of practice (figuratively resembling a spider weaving its web) the designer creates an interconnected structure. This 'woven web' should be regarded, not as a single centralised structure, but as a network, with many interconnected nodes. The designer's continuous interaction between the nodes (the different perspectives) is key for continuous progression and knowledge development. Hansson highlighted that interactions between local and global nodes (perspectives) can help to shape the scope of a network, and described how focusing on local interactions can ultimately lead to global connections.[7]

Helena noted that gaps will appear when 'weaving' the web—voids—representing the unknown: knowledge that is yet to be explored. These void-areas are therefore not empty but hold the potential for further discovery.[8] As such, when this type of exploratory mode of 'weaving' is in progress, the designer's continuous movement across the web feeds its scope: an ever-growing, decentralised network, filled with opportunity.

> ...my participatory designer role has been primarily to act as a 'connector,' someone who explores opportunities in connecting disparate elements. ...weaving, tracing, and exploring the connections and voids...borrowing ideas, translating them to be redesigned in a different context.[9]

The many analogies found in these conceptual approaches helped to broaden my understanding of academic research, and bring new light to my own work. Yet, the deep dive into the complex, hard-to-understand, and unfamiliar field of academia often felt overwhelming. I sought to break down the concepts used in Hansson's research by going back to basics: one of its major aspects is centred around collaboration.

As such, deciphering methods to enable translation and exchange amongst collaborators is key. Hansson's use of Actor-Network Theory[10] acted as the foundation for the conceptual frameworks applied in her research.

Layered and multifaceted, the way I wrapped my head around Actor-Network Theory was by understanding it as a set of ideas—a series of theoretical concepts—originating from social science that views society as 'an ongoing achievement',[11] as 'something that is constantly in the making.'[12] ANT aims to provide analytical tools for explaining how society (and its norms) are formed,[13] and how power and agency within it are *performed*.[14] It aims to explain the continuous interactions and relational ties between the elements that build a specific 'system/network'—meaning, help to decipher the social structure between collaborators from different disciplines or explore the factors that drive a site-specific craft. Actor-Network Theory simply becomes a way into the said 'system/network', allowing researchers to thoroughly explore its constituent parts.[15]

BOUNDARY OBJECT

During our conversation, the topic of the designer as a 'weaver' was prefaced by me asking Hansson about the concept of the Boundary Object[16] in relation to her research. To my limited prior knowledge, Hansson added that a boundary object is an ANT-related concept: used in her research as a framework for discussion, to better understand collaborative complexities.[17] Hansson described how a boundary object is made up of various elements that are understood differently from different perspectives. Helena explained that in a collaborative context, the boundary object can be spatial rather than physical—it can be a shared space that acts as a bridge between two distinct communities collaborating on a common task.

Its meaning and purpose are flexible enough for each perspective to use it according to their own specific needs, yet robust enough to maintain its core identity, so that each perspective can recognise it as the same 'thing'.[18]

Hansson highlighted that it is through the collaborative process itself that the boundary object comes to be, as it cannot be determined beforehand. Meaning, that a boundary object—spatial or physical—can help to facilitate collaborative processes without hierarchy between different perspectives collaborating:

> ...the BO concept acknowledges that people are different and have different ideas and approaches. Rather than speaking with one voice, it asserts that different voices ought to be heard, thus encouraging non-consensus. At the same time, BO provides suggestions for how to deal with these differences.[19]

I was curious about the direct link between slöjd and the boundary object. Historically, in Hedared, slöjd was a means to an end. Basket making was practised out of necessity. When asked, 'Can the concept of the boundary object reveal today's need for slöjd in design?', the short answer was, 'Yes'. Hansson expressed the idea of using slöjd itself as a boundary object, describing it as a process that fosters dialogue when collaborating. More than a physical object, slöjd should be regarded as a process—a tool for comprehension, reflection, and an opportunity for interaction between different disciplines or social spaces. Hansson likened it to the historical 'thing' in Germanic societies, where communities gathered to resolve disagreements and communal issues.

In the scope of her research, a 'slöjd thing' allows people to jointly reflect on complex topics, and find new language to comprehend and articulate abstract ideas, by engaging in a tangible process. Helena noted that although slöjd practitioners make concrete, tangible objects, they often lack reflective space: time, or an environment open to critical reflection. Such reflective spaces are necessary to, for example, fully understand slöjd's potential in design or its potential in making abstract and hard-to-understand issues like sustainability more comprehensive.

The fundamental elements of a slöjd process, as described by Hansson, can be broken down into two things:

material and technique. In the example of the Hedared basket: the intricate task of its material acquisition is paired with the technical aspect of constructing the actual object.

Together with instructions on how these two elements work together, Hansson explained how a slow process commences for the practitioner, where the body works in unison with the mind, to connect these dots; how the right grip of the knife feels in one's hand to allow the annual rings to 'evenly split' across their full length. As these components are concrete, and their procedures visible (i.e. extracted annual rings, woven into a basket), a slöjd process can be regarded as a language within itself. It is not solely reliant on spoken language to be understood, for the individual practitioner, or between collaborators—muscle memory allows one to slowly demonstrate with the body, and communicate by doing.

I related this to my experience working with Curt Bengtsson in Risa. When he demonstrated the material process of the basket, the many unspoken physical cues made its methodology more comprehensible, first through observation, then by handling the material myself. Through the visual and the tactile, a deeper understanding of the process' various dimensions and complexities formed.

Contrary to handicraft, Hansson described design as a less transparent making process, one that requires a certain prior knowledge and specific tools to succeed. At the time of our conversation, viewed through the lens of my then-current curriculum, it could be argued that design relies on understanding specific contexts to be successful: who the textile is for, how it should function and where it will be used. Once these variables are identified, the material and making process adapts and proceeds accordingly.

Hansson continued to describe how the practice of slöjd allows a series of relationalities to form between the craft's local surroundings—its immediate social, economic, or environmental context, and the conditions of the greater world surrounding it. I continued to draw parallels to the basket, reflecting on how its material acquisition process provides insights into its site-specific ecology, the lineage of its makers, the environmental factors shaping its future practice, and the role its practitioners play within this ever-evolving kaleido-scope.

Answering my initial query: the core principles of slöjd share liminal qualities with the framework of the boundary object, as both are methods to facilitate collaboration, dialogue and development. Within the scope of Hansson's design-led research, both can simply help to explain things.

***

The introduction to theory and its 'conceptual strategies' acted as fuel to my existing research. While its concepts offered valuable insights that deepened my understanding of my own research, I quickly became aware of its (potentially problematic) complexities, particularly when addressing cultural or social issues. This only deepened my interest in exploring where my research could find a place within the landscape of established theoretical frameworks. During the same period as my theoretical discoveries, the online seminar *Skogsklok* ('Forest Wise') was held, initiated by the Cultural Administration in the region of Västra Götaland. Its mission was to bring together various perspectives on 'the forest's untapped slöjd potential'.[20]

The invited speakers included landowners, slöjd practitioners, conservators, designers, and researchers such as Helena Hansson. Ecologist Pella Thiel was also among them. During her talk, 'Time to Renegotiate Our View of Nature?', Thiel argued that slöjd can play a vital role in a modern-day paradigm shift—one in which the legal recognition of Nature as a living entity is crucial for creating true sustainable development.

Thiel argued that from a Westernised, human-centred perspective, the assumption has been made that humans are separate from Nature and all its living beings—placed at the top of a hierarchical scale and therefore able to claim dominion over other forms of life, treating them as resources to be consumed. In short, Thiel explained that the legal recognition of Nature is essential, as we humans depend on healthy ecosystems for our own survival. She argued that the same ethical principles that justify human rights should apply to Nature, highlighting the paradox that a man-made 'thing' like a corporation has legal rights, while a *living* entity like Nature does not.[21]

Thiel continued to describe how the industrialisation of Swedish forests has led to a general environmental homogenisation, reducing the biodiversity crucial for thriving ecosystems. As a result, complex forest environments have been replaced by uniform landscapes, where forests have become scenes of 'the same trees, of the same age—made into the same type of planks.'[22]

Agneta Boqvist, author of the paper 'The Hidden Economy' (1978), presents similar arguments made in the mid-nineteenth century that oppose and question 'modern development' in relation to the forest. The reports she presents expands on how the increasing exploitation of woodland resources affected residents in Sjuhärad: '...the forests are heavily used every year, to the extent that many households now barely find enough forest for the needs of the household.'[23]

Building on these concerns, Boqvist also includes later statements made from the early twentieth century, highlighting how local slöjd practices were being affected, as the rapid felling of trees had made it increasingly difficult to source specific timber required in certain practices.[24]

Another prime example is the continued difficulty in finding adequate material needed to practice the Hedared basket's material technique. The ideal pine tree needs to have grown undisturbed for nearly a century. The narrator of the documentary *Basketry from Hedared* (1978) reflects on the issue of material acquisition, echoing the arguments made by Thiel and the earlier reports presented by Boqvist: '...it has become increasingly difficult to find suitable material to supply the making of the Hedared basket. Trees sown in modern forestry grow too quickly, making the distance between the annual rings too great.'[25] Most notably, the film raises the same issue a century after the initial report emerged and, evidently, still bears relevance almost half a century after its release.

Thiel continued: in Western societies, with strong established infrastructures, the meaning of development often gets confused; modern ideas of development no longer align with ideas of progression. The concept of development in an industrialised context has become the very reason for the deterioration of the living ecosystems we depend on. Thiel described that acknowledging Nature as a subject would allow for, not only sustainable development, but *true* progression. She mentions the symbiotic relationship found between Nature and Indigenous knowledges around the world, and references 'The Honourable Harvest', in short:

> Know the ways of the ones who take care of you, so that you may take care of them... Give thanks for what you have been given. Give a gift, in reciprocity for what you have taken. Sustain the ones who sustain you...[26]

As found in the craftsmanship of the Hedared basket, its site-specific practice arose from the villagers' deep knowledge of the forest: their immediate surroundings. The basket asks its practitioner to familiarise, respect, and know the ways from which it can continue to be. *Att korga* ('to basket') continues to represent a long-lasting synergy between humans and Nature and remains a symbol for the vital bond between maker and material.

A THOUGHT ON KNOWLEDGE

Design for me as a young queer kid was the idea of grandeur, something other, unknown, it represented the vastness of an unseen world. It felt like a distant, uncharted truth hidden behind a concrete-poured curtain, only existing beyond linoleum-covered floors. As I've grown older, more pragmatic, and begun to understand the greater contexts in which design is practised, I still find myself primarily interested in approaching design from the perspective of it being something of an enigma, something beyond reach—an exploration of a distant unknown that aims to acquire the much sought-after purpose when making.

The core of my cultural awareness comes from my immediate surroundings: from growing up in Hulta. In my experience, neither the recognisable rurality of Västgötska nor the concrete-poured 'newness' of Förortssvenska adheres to knowledge as found in a book.

> Being a queer person with roots in both Sweden and Tunisia, I naturally have an extensive view of the world, anchored in the belief that inclusivity and representation matter, especially when it comes to issues of unsustainable development.

Knowledge, as I knew it, was soured by doing: observing and navigating cultural spaces. It continues to be how I per-ceive, recognise and value knowledge today. Having the priv-ilege to study abroad, this point of view extends in wanting to provide space for the social and cultural context I come from— to articulate how its collective experiences are valid, and its perspectives bear weight; within the cemented context of slöjd, the general culture of Västgötska, or in the homogeneous spac-es that a Bachelor's in design would prove to be. Creating space for its perspectives translates into a felt urgency to re-examine outdated perceptions and practices: when devising approaches to industrial processes as a student, or when working with the established traditions of slöjd.

In the narrow scope of tradition, I find even more ur-gency, not to overlook how the realities of others can, not only challenge, but more so, enrich old and entrenched views.

The purely decorative becomes subpar without ac-knowledging that nothing exists in a vacuum, that any practice has social and cultural dimensions to consider.

> One was often challenged to devise approaches to industrial conundrums and regularly invited by tutors to question standardised processes of

making deemed unsustainable due to environmental reasons. Students on the course were encouraged to approach such issues holistically, using their own field within textiles (which in my case was the medium of weaving) as a tool to do so.

The introduction of theory played a major part in rationalising and aligning these thoughts, to connect the abstract: a felt need, with the tangible: a composition of colour and texture. Coming from a 'young culture' built into a 'faceless' environment, theoretical frameworks presented as a familiar type of awareness, one that is foreign to my inherent relationship to knowledge. Similarly to Västgötska, I experienced its introduction as akin to the expected ability of understanding how to navigate both known and unspoken cultural cues: to not deviate from what supposedly is appropriate, proper and fitting—lagom.

Theoretical frameworks felt synonymous with a universal understanding of the world, one that doesn't translate to a faceless environment. I wonder if discovering theory, and wanting to speak its 'language', connects me to my younger self: of knowing that the world is greater (beyond parabolic antennas attached to concrete-poured balconies).

I wonder if wanting to procure knowledge from its 'conceptual frameworks' is an extension of my own continuous search, if its familiar sense of expectation has become a gateway to continue approaching design from the perceived idea of it being something other and unknown (that holds the vastness of an unseen world).

In that fleeting thought, I realise that the experience of living on linoleum-covered floors continues to hold its own intrinsic value. Hulta shares its collective bits of knowledge with its people; embodying its wisdom is a reality that grants a sense of purpose that will always go beyond the realm of the purely decorative, and instead of being inferior, its lived experiences are what fuel the gains of the ideas found in theoretical concepts.

***

...development is not a result of an individual designer's work. Nor is it a quick fix, but rather a slow process that emerges and develops over time. The weaving practice means that I am part of a 'developmental continuum' that is constantly shifting...[27]

In the late 1990s, when commencing her practice as a postgraduate in Industrial Design, Hansson mentioned experiencing a polarisation between design and slöjd.

Designers would often view slöjd as something old and irrelevant. In the same way, slöjd practitioners would think that design has nothing to do with their work and that designers knew nothing about tradition or materials. During our conversation, Helena described her students as being part of a paradigm shift, where their quest for authenticity colours the curriculum, and is reflected in the increasingly conceptual projects.

While Lennart, historically, was introduced to, and dealt with slöjd through necessity, Hansson describes seeing a need for a younger generation of designers to find purpose in their practice. Processes of slöjd combined with theoretical frameworks can give weight to its contemporary use in design, beyond compositions of colour and texture—when wanting to holistically encompass the interiority of the self, with one's relationality to the outside world—slöjd together with theory can simply help to explain things.

NOTES

1. Hemslöjd
    'Craft-based production of utility or decorative objects, originating in the home; for personal
    use or with the intention of selling.'
    Svenska Akademien (2009) *Svensk ordbok A–L*, first edition.
    Stockholm: Svenska Akademien, p. 1180. Translated by the author.

Beyond its definition, hemslöjd was shaped by broader cultural and historical movements, particularly the efforts to preserve Swedish traditions and cultural heritage during the late 19th and early
20th centuries. For additional context:

    1.1. 'What today is regarded as hemslöjd has, to a great extent, been defined by the
    Hemslöjds movement.[1.2] The ideas of preservation, taste cultivation, help-to-self-
    help, and aesthetics that inspired those involved in the movement around the
    turn of the last century, were not an isolated phenomenon but rather part of a much
    larger movement in society. The turn of the 20th century is often characterised as
    a time of change on multiple levels. A series of radical transformations of the 'old
    allmoge society' during the second half of the 19th century such as land reforms,
    compulsory schooling, new means of communication, and newspaper reading,
    led many in the intellectual elite to identify the need for a rescue mission to
    safeguard Swedish traditions.[1.3] Involved in this effort were social movements such
    as Hemslöjden and Hembygdsrörelsen, as well as cultural-historical, regional- and
    open-air museums. Engaged were also researchers in the academic fields of ethnol-
    ogy and archaeology, which developed alongside the rescue efforts, to preserve and
    describe the disappearing agrarian Sweden.', Hyltén-Cavallius, C. (2015)
    'Att göra en nation'. In: *Konsthantverk i Sverige*, Part 1, (Eds.), Zetterlund, C., Hyltén-
    Cavallius, C., Rosenqvist, J. Tumba: Mångkulturellt centrum, p. 23.

    1.2. This article is partly built on my thesis *Traditionens estetik. Spelet mellan
    inhemsk och internationell hemslöjd* (Stockholm: Carlsson, 2007), partly on
    the project "Crafting identity. Identification, aesthetics and minority politics
    in sámi duodji". See Charlotte Hyltén-Cavallius, "Om organisering av äkthet,
    erkännande och identifikation i sámi duodji", in: Katarina Ek-Nilsson &
    Birgitta Meurling (ed.), *Talande ting. Berättelser och materialitet*, (Uppsala:
    Institutet för språk och folkminnen, 2014).

    1.3. See Agneta Lilja, *Föreställningen om den ideala uppteckningen. En studie
    av idé och praktik vid traditionssamlande arkiv. Ett exempel från Uppsala
    1914–1945*, Diss. (Uppsala, 1996); Catharina Lundström, *Fruars makt och
    omakt. Kön, klass och kulturarv 1900–1940*, Diss. (Umeå, 2005); Bo G. Nilsson,
    *Folkhemmets arbetarminnen. En undersökning av de historiska och diskursi-
    va villkoren för svenska arbetares levnadsskildringar*, Diss. (Stockholm, 1996).

2. Allmoge
    'The peasant population of a country.'
    Allmoge culture
    'Cultural activities practised by the peasant population,
    often to emphasise origin and in contrast to so-called high culture.'
    Svenska Akademien (2009) *Svensk ordbok A–L*, first edition. Stockholm: Svenska Akademien,
    p. 41. Translated by the author.

Building on the definition of hemslöjd, the concept of allmoge played a key role in shaping the
aesthetic and cultural values that influenced the hemslöjds movement:

    2.1 'Allmoge culture was seen as 'a reservoir of domestic traditions from prehisto-
    ric times and the Middle Ages', and it appeared as static and unchanging.', Nilsson,
    Folkhemmets arbetarminnen, p. 53, cited in Hyltén-Cavallius, C. (2015) 'Att
    göra en nation'. In: *Konsthantverk i Sverige*, Part 1, (Eds.), Zetterlund, C., Hyltén-
    Cavallius, C., Rosenqvist, J. Tumba: Mångkulturellt centrum, p. 24.
    Translated by the author.

    2.2 'Hemslöjden generally considered old allmoge patterns as belonging to what was
    beautiful. That which was ugly was instead found in things associated with the new,

259

the modern...', Hyltén-Cavallius, C. (2015) 'Att göra en nation'. In: *Konsthantverk i Sverige*, Part 1, (Eds.), Zetterlund, C., Hyltén-Cavallius, C., Rosenqvist, J. Tumba: Mångkulturellt centrum, p. 27–28. Translated by the author.

3.   In 1955 slöjd was made a compulsory subject in Swedish schools, having been common in the curriculum since the turn of the last century.[3.1] It is still today included in formal education, and was described in the late 1800s by pioneering slöjd educator Otto Salomon, who stated:

'The value of the Slöjd as an educational means is, comparatively speaking, many-sided. Beside the skill to turn the hand to useful labor, which is taught the children to their undeniable advantage, it is also capable, in other ways of assisting to a notable extent in the development of various powers and qualities valuable in after life. Among these are to be mentioned love for labor, and, as a direct consequence, industry and persistence. Self-reliance, exactness and attentiveness are other characteristics that are demanded in the Slöjd, and, accordingly, also attain development through it.', Salomon, O. (1888) *The Slöjd in the Service of the School.* Translated by W. H. Carpenter. New York: Industrial Education Association, pp. 185–186.

The distinction between slöjd as a educational means and the mission of the Hemslöjds movement was significant according to Salomon:

'...Slöjd instruction is divided, into two different movements, which, although confused by superficial observers, in reality have nothing in common except the name. The one is of purely national-economical significance, in that it is based upon the fact that domestic industry is decreasing more and more, and sets itself the task of taking measures to teach the rural population, especially fitting Slöjd labors for home occupation, whose products may be applied either in the house itself, or may serve directly for sale. This Slöjd movement sees in the school the means for extending Slöjd skill. [...] The objects produced become the essential part; the worker himself, on the other hand, is an incidental part. [...] It is wholly different with the other movement that desires to place the Slöjd in the service of the school. Manual labor arranged on pedagogical principles is, in many respects, an extremely efficient means for the education of children. It desires, therefore, to introduce the Slöjd into the school, not for the furtherance of the Slöjd, but because it believes that the school, by means of this branch of study, will exert an influence, in a manner more perfect and as many-sided as is possible, upon the development of its pupils. Not the products of labor, but the laborers themselves are, according to this idea, the most important part.', Salomon, O. (1888) *The Slöjd in the Service of the School.* Translated by W. H. Carpenter. New York: Industrial Education Association, pp. 181–182.

   3.1 Borg, K. (2016) In: *Tilde—Tema slöjd: nordisk forskning, bedömning och läroplaner.* Rapport nr 16. Umeå: Umeå Universitet, p. 33.

4.   King Karl X Gustav (March Across the Belts, 1658).
5.   'The Bocksten Man's costume is one of Europe's best preserved garments from the Middle Ages. The costume is dated from the period 1350–1370 [...] The clothes are made from woven wool that was processed to become 'wadmal'—a coarse, dense woollen fabric that is warm and rain-resistant. The outfit is the only one of its kind found in Europe.', Halland Museum of Cultural History (2024) *The Bocksten Man's unique outfit.*
      https://museumhalland.se/en/the-bocksten-man/the-bocksten-mans-outfit/ [20/06/2024].
6.   Global Footprint Network. (n.d.). *About Earth Overshoot Day.*
      https://overshoot.footprintnetwork.org/about-earth-overshoot-day/ [20/06/2024].
7.   'Recognizing that the world is interconnected is of great importance when discussing sustainable global development. We need to understand that our local actions, which occur in a particular situation at a specific time, are influenced by and affect other people's actions conducted elsewhere in another context.', Hansson (2021), p. 70.
8.   'As design scholar Yoko Akama (2015), who is inspired by Latour (2005, 2010), suggests, a void is not just an empty space in the network. It should instead be seen as a kind of 'plasma' that has also agency; according to Latour (2005), plasma is 'that which is not yet formatted, not measured, not yet socialized, not yet engaged in metrological chains, and not yet covered, surveyed, mobilized, or subjectified.' (p. 244)', cited in Hansson (2021), p. 71.
9.   'When looking back on the process, I can see that my participatory designer role has been primarily to act as a 'connector,' someone who explores opportunities in connecting disparate elements. A challenge with this role is that the designer often becomes 'the network prince' (Storni, 2015, p. 167). I therefore suggest a humbler role, which I explain as the weaver. This kind of designer-actor is constantly moving around in the net, weaving, tracing, and exploring the

connections and voids in the work-net, borrowing ideas, translating them to be redesigned in a different context.', Hansson (2021), p. 192.

10. Latour, B. (2005) *Reassembling the Social: An Introduction to Actor-Network Theory*. Oxford: University Press.

11. 'One of the core assumptions of ANT is that what the social sciences usually call "society" is an ongoing achievement. ANT is an attempt to provide analytical tools for explaining the very process by which society is constantly reconfigured. What distinguishes it from other constructivist approaches is its explanation of society in the making, in which science and technology play a key part. (Callon, 2001, p. 62)', cited in Hansson (2021), p. 65.

12. Hansson (2021), p. 64.

13. Ibid.

14. Ibid., p. 65.

15. 'Czarniawska (2016) suggests that ANT should be seen as a method or "guide" for how to study associations (p. 166). In this case, ANT acts as both a conceptual framework and a research methodology used to explore "how networks are built or assembled and maintained to achieve a specific objective" (Carroll et al., 2012, p. 4).', cited in Hansson, H. (2021), p. 64.

16. Leigh Star, S. and Griesemer, J.R. (1989) 'Institutional Ecology, 'Translations' and Boundary Objects: Amateurs and Professionals in Berkeley's Museum of Vertebrate Zoology, 1907-39', In: *Social Studies of Science*, Volume 19—Issue 3.

17. 'It is not a line on a map but rather an unexplored territory where different people meet to negotiate their different views, which is done with support from BOs.', Hansson (2021), p. 68.

18. 'Boundary objects are both plastic enough to adapt to local needs and constraints of the several parties employing them, yet robust enough to maintain a common identity across sites. They are weakly structured in common use and become strongly structured in individual site use. They may be abstract or concrete. They have different meanings in different social worlds, but their structure is common enough to more than one world to make them recognizable, a means of translation. (Star and Griesemer 1989, p. 393)', quoted in Hansson (2021), p. 68.

19. Seravalli (2014), cited in Hansson (2021), p. 68.

20. Kulturförvaltningen VGR (2021) *Skogsklok*. https://www.vgregion.se/f/kulturforvaltningen/vi-erbjuder/fortbildning/inspelade-webbinari-er-och-foredrag/skogsklok2/ [20/05/2022]. Translated by the author.

21. Ibid.

22. Ibid.

23. Länsmansrapp. (1866–1870), quoted in Boqvist, A. (1978) *Den Dolda Ekonomin—En etnologisk studie av Näringsstrukturen i Bollebygd 1850–1950*. Lund: LiberLäromedel/Gleerup, p. 24. Translated by the author.

24. Hemslöjdskommitténs betänkande: del 2 (1918), cited in Boqvist (1978), p. 24.

25. Jansson, I. (1978) *Slöjd från Sjuhärad: Korgslöjd i Hedared*. Borås: Slöjd i Väst/De sju härader-nas hemslöjdsförening/Kulturförvaltningen VGR. Translated by the author.

26. 'The guidelines for the Honorable Harvest are not written down, or even consistently spoken of as a whole—they are reinforced in small acts of daily life. But if you were to list them, they might look something like this:
Know the ways of the ones who take care of you, so that you
may take care of them.
Introduce yourself. Be accountable as the one who comes
asking for life.
Ask permission before taking. Abide by the answer.
Never take the first. Never take the last.
Take only what you need.
Take only that which is given.
Never take more than half. Leave some for others.
Harvest in a way that minimizes harm.
Use it respectfully. Never waste what you have taken.
Share.
Give thanks for what you have been given.
Give a gift, in reciprocity for what you have taken.
Sustain the ones who sustain you and the earth will last
forever.'
Wall Kimmerer, R. (2020) *Braiding Sweetgrass: Indigenous Wisdom, Scientific Knowledge and the Teachings of Plants*. London: Penguin Books Limited, p. 183.

27. Hansson (2021), p. 192.

Almevik, G. (2016) 'From Archive to Living Heritage—Participatory Documentation Methods in Crafts'. In: Palmsköld, A., Rosenqvist, J., Almevik, G. (Eds.), *Crafting Cultural Heritage*. Gothenburg: University of Gothenburg, pp. 77–99.

Benn S., Edwards M., Angus-Leppan T. (2013) 'Organizational Learning and the Sustainability Community of Practice: The Role of Boundary Objects'. In: *Organization & Environment*, Volume 26—Issue 2, pp. 184–202.

Berry, T. (2006) *Evening Thoughts: Reflecting on Earth as a Sacred Community*. San Francisco: Sierra Club Books.

Bowker, G.C., and Leigh Star, S. (1999) *Sorting Things Out: Classification and Its Consequences*. Massachusetts: The MIT Press.

Cullinan, C. (2003) *Wild Law: A Manifesto for Earth Justice*. Cambridge: Green Books.

Lupo, E. and Giunta, E. (2016) 'Contemporary Authentic: a Design Driven Strategy for Activating Intangible Heritage and Craft Knowledge'. In: Palmsköld, A., Rosenqvist, J., Almevik, G. (Eds.), *Crafting Cultural Heritage*. Gothenburg: University of Gothenburg, pp. 55–74.

Nash, R.F. (1989) *The Rights of Nature: A History of Environmental Ethics*. Wisconsin: The University of Wisconsin Press.

Stone, C.D. (2010) *Should Trees Have Standing? Essays on Law, Morals, and the Environment*. Oxford: Oxford University Press.

von Busch, O. (2010) 'Exploring Net Political Craft: From Collective to Connective'. In: *Craft Research*, Volume 1—Issue 1, pp. 113–124.

von Busch, O. (2012) 'Generation Open: Contested Creativity and Capabilities'. In: *The Design Journal: An International Journal for All Aspects of Design*, Volume 15—Issue 4, pp. 443–459.

BEING AND BECOMING: REFLECTIONS OF A WEAVER

MARCIA HARVEY ISAKSSON

SOMEONE REFERRED TO ME as a textile artist recently. I mulled over the epithet for a while, wondering when I had become that which they perceived me to be. True: I make art. Also true: I use textile methods and, at times, textile materials in the art-making process. But does that make me a textile artist?

Or am I an artist who works *through* textiles?

A triviality, you may say—but I liken it to being called an immigrant and not an expatriate—it's a question of nuance. Being a black woman living in Sweden, the first assumption when being perceived is that I am an immigrant, probably a refugee here solely to benefit from the Swedish welfare system. Counterparts of Western descent are readily accepted as expats contributing to both the cosmopolitan feel and the tax income of the country. At first glance, I may appear to be a textile artist but that is only one way of viewing who I am and what I do. The truth is I despise being pigeonholed. I reserve the right to change my mind and to reinvent myself as I see fit. Labels carry connotations that tend to stick and restrict.

Now don't get me wrong, I take it as a compliment to be referred to as a textile artist. I dedicated eight years of my life to making space for textile and fiber art, craft and design through my arena Fiberspace. A wonderful time that gave me access to the rich and varied world of textiles, allowing me to run the gamut of practices from technical nerds to conceptual thinkers to experimental pioneers and many hybrids.

So, to be included in that very special sort of practitioner is an honour, because textile artists have taught me many things, among others: the value of craft and inherited knowledge; how skill and deep thought can be combined to create transcendent works; the importance of paying attention to details that other people do not necessarily see, like the backside of works or the mounting methods. Though Fiberspace has now given way to Southnord; a platform I founded in 2023, focused on making space for the creative output of visual artists of African descent situated in the Nordics; I carry these lessons over into my wider practice and my life in general. Nevertheless, the title of textile artist does not sit well with me—like a sweater that shrunk in the wash, I feel it boxing me in, restricting my movement, holding me in check. Perhaps textile explorer would suit me better. Less imposter syndrome, more room to manoeuvre.

The state of being is, for me, a state of inertia and continuity. It is a state to rest in, to be comfortable in, persisting in the familiar. Perhaps that is why I resist 'being' a textile artist—if 'being' is the state then I prefer being a textile explorer. It is through the exploration of textile traditions, techniques and materials that I come closer to a state that suits my nature better, that fluid ever-changing state of becoming.

My textile knowledge is deeply rooted in my mother's love for knitting and her habit of getting all her clothes tailor-made. The first textile technique I learned was crocheting, an accessible skill, easy for my right-handed mother to teach my left-handed five-year-old self. I came to discover, through the amateur and the domestic, that the imagination is key to realising the full potential of any textile project. Later in life, as an adult living in Stockholm, far from my childhood home in Harare, I revisited my textile interest through a short weaving course, and it had me hooked. The combination of mathematical rationality and visceral tactility ignited curiosity in both my brain halves. The exotic nature of the craft itself was also appealing. Never had I encountered a loom, in all my years growing up in Zimbabwe; but here in Sweden, they were a dime-a-dozen, being given away for free just to be saved from bonfires.

The Swedish society had become so far removed from its agrarian past that the skill of weaving, once an integral societal skill, had been relegated to distant memories of great-grandmothers and grandmothers weaving for household needs or as a mere hobby. Sweden's societal evolution and its thirst for modernity has had it chasing the fifth industrial revolution and beyond, actively eroding craft's cultural importance. Schoolchildren in Sweden have a mere fifty hours of craft education per year. Who needs craft when we have AI?—that seems to be the general sentiment of policymakers. The specific practical and cultural knowledges held in a tool such as the loom, are in danger of dying out if not passed on. Without these alternate ways of knowing and learning, how well-equipped will human beings be to adapt to an uncertain future?

Weavers in the West (2018) Museum of Ethnography.
Film still: JungJiea Hung.

Some years after my first encounter with the loom, I decided to travel to Kyoto and immerse myself in the long-standing tradition of Japanese Ikat weaving—a very precise and methodical skill that, within the cultural setting, demanded absolute adherence to accepted norms and practices. While in Japan, I experienced a reverence for craft in general, and for textiles in particular, that I have never experienced anywhere else in the world. The unique presence and remaining cultural significance of textiles in Japan, single-handedly inspired my decision to start Fiberspace, and influenced my curatorial approach to the platform. After having learnt some hard lessons during the Ikat weaving process, about how cutting corners in preparation work comes back to bite you later, I returned to Sweden with the understanding that you need to know the rules well in order to break them successfully. A lesson that has served me well in my later exploration of looms and the weaving apparatus, when moving my practice out of the studio and into the public arena.

The next stage in my development as a weaver came from becoming an apprentice to a Gambian/Senegalese weaving master, who happened to live in Sweden. I did a crash course in the West African strip-weaving tradition using drag-stone looms, that are typically constructed and used outdoors. My master, Ousman Sarr, had learnt the skill from his father, who had learnt it from his, and so on and so forth, through generations. Generally, the narrow strip looms were reserved for professional weavers—men. Women spun and dyed the thread. In some parts of West Africa, the upright loom was used in the home by women making fabric to clothe their own families. According to Ousman, there are more and more young women learning narrow strip weaving, however the overall number of new apprentices is dwindling. The youth prefer other careers today.

What drew me to this model of loom was its architecture and the geographical reasons connected to its appearance. The loom is cleverly constructed by tying together upright, horizontal and diagonal poles into a frame that holds the heart of the loom, the heddles and beater. The frame was traditionally made from saplings harvested from the surrounding area, making the actual loom (i.e. the heddles and beater) extremely portable,

Dialogue (2020) Västerås Konstmuseum. Photo: Marcia Harvey Isaksson.

Weave Weft Woven (2024) Röhsska Museum of Design and Craft.
Photo: Kristin Lidell.

allowing professional weavers to be nomadic. Weaving in West Africa is commonly done outdoors, thanks to the agreeable climate, which explains why the warp can be stretched out at such a great distance. The traditional Swedish loom has been developed to suit the conditions of a northern climate—a compact knock-down kit that keeps the warp wrapped tight. Each tool revealing something about the place it was conceived.

During the apprenticeship, my previous experience with written literature on (Swedish) weaving traditions was replaced by an oral and demonstrational transfer of knowledge. I learnt by watching, listening, doing and asking. I learnt that some knowledge is non-linear and of the body, not of the mind. I also learnt that my interest lies more in the loom (and its process), than in the woven textile. I am fascinated by the construction and the quintessential elements required for a loom to function as a tool for production. It is through the loom I can explore my interest in examining the similarities and differences in global weaving traditions. It is through the loom I can delve into how traditional practices have developed through human interactions and examine what traces these exchanges have left in the loom. It is here I become curious on what looms evoke in those encountering them in public spaces and the ensuing conversations.

The first time I wove in public was on my drag-stone loom at the Museum of Ethnography in Stockholm. I had decided that the best way to bring their collection of African textiles to life was to weave one of my own within the confines of the museum walls. My apprenticeship with Ousman had been a necessary part of my preparations for this, my first performance weaving. While I wove, I reflected on how artefacts from the Global South have ended up in Western museums and how much knowledge and cultural context has been lost by their removal from their place of origin. I felt that the simple act of building an authentic narrow strip loom and weaving a narrow strip fabric while in dialogue with the museum's visitors was a way of filling in a few of those gaps.

The narrow strip loom is a living heritage to be used, not an artefact to be preserved in perpetuity.

The next time my drag-stone loom made a public appearance was at Västerås Konstmuseum, where I had connected it to my Swedish counterbalance loom. They shared a warp that could be woven simultaneously on both looms and as the warp was transformed into cloth, the looms came closer and closer together until they met in the middle. Their physical appearances may have been strikingly different, but their functionality and working principles are the same. Much like us humans.

The latest installation of the looms was at the Röhsska Museum in Gothenburg. Not only were my two original looms still in dialogue; I added a third to the mix—an upright loom that borrowed the drag-stone loom's love of out-stretched warps. The warp was free to interact with the high ceilings and the tall walls of the space, the architecture of the loom in dialogue with the architecture of the building. Each new project brings new knowledge to my practice. It was through my teachers I learnt how to weave, but it is through the loom I truly became a weaver. It is through the loom my textile exploration of traditions, techniques and materials continues, allowing me to come closer to my true nature, in the ever-changing state of becoming.

Marcia Harvey Isaksson (b. 1975, Zimbabwe) is an artist and curator based in Stockholm. In her artistic practice she uses weaving and other textile methods to investigate cultural and personal heritage, the transfer of knowledge over generations, and how narratives of the past effect the present and the future. She is interested in site-specific narratives, working often with a mix of media, from sculpture to performance. Harvey Isaksson is also the founder of Southnord, a platform whose purpose is to make space for black and Afro-Nordic artists. She previously ran Fiberspace (2015–2023), an arena for textile art, handicrafts and design.

THE ~~LAST~~ BASKET MAKER(S) AND I

CURT BENGTSSON (b. 1949) now carries on the legacy of the basket. His knowledge has been invaluable to me. Curt patiently went through each step of the basket's material process whilst answering questions, posing for photos and sharing anecdotes of his own basket-related experiences. We began our endeavour by wandering the woods in Risa, together with Ulla Petterson. I had the privilege of witnessing his artisanal skills in action on the very land Lennart had once lived and similarly roamed to find proper timber to use. As I documented and recorded, Curt walked from tree to tree, knocking off small pieces of bark, to see how the fibres of each tree lay.

Searching for the one that is *rätklöven*.

Having continued working closely with Bengtsson has given insights into what it's like being the 'last maker'. Lennart's inaugural period of holding the title was brief and is of legend through storytelling (least of all within the pages of this publication). But with Curt, the heritage is live and direct, I get to see history repeat itself where the epithet has found yet another maker to be bestowed its honour. Although never explicitly expressed, his sense of duty permeates our interactions.

Bengtsson would return to Risa on several occasions, and each time, we would go through a new section of the material process until the day he brought pine planks ready for the 'extraction' process of their annual rings. We sat on the porch at Ulla's house (that formerly belonged to Lennart), where I helplessly tried to get the annual rings to 'evenly split' across their full length. I managed to split one or two on my own before Curt helped me to finish the remaining.

During this period, I, through Curt, got in contact with Knut Östgård, another prominent figure within the wood-slöjd world in Sweden. Knut (b. 1944) together with Tore Fagersson, were the two slöjdare featured in the documentary *Basketry in Hedared* (1978), as Lennart's apprentices. My first point of contact with Knut was through email. After I had introduced my research, I asked Knut about his experience with the basket, and he responded with:

275

Hi Fadhel!

I had received a scholarship from Lerum's hemslöjds association which enabled me to do a course with Lennart for a week. The handicraft advisors Svea Landén and Ingrid Strömvall then wanted me to participate in the filming of the Hedared basket that Ingemar Jansson did.

The film is available at the advisors' office in Borås. I worked with the basket for a few years and led courses in Hedared, where I had Gustav Persson as a student. He was so talented, and as it turned out, he had worked with the basket in his younger years. Rune Holm was another talented basket maker who made large mangle baskets. During the 1980s, I sat at the Liljevalchs anniversary exhibition and wove baskets. I was then invited to Konstfack in Stockholm to show how the splitting of the material and the basket weaving was done. Some of the students wanted to try and explore the possibility of using the material in their studies.

I have used the same material for other types of baskets I have made. The ways to look for, and find material in the forest is an important feature in my slöjd and is something I learned from Lennart. In my courses, I try to pass this on.

Regards,
Knut Östgård

We then had a phone call. Knut spoke more in detail about his experience working in Risa and described Lennart as a kind, timid, and modest man. He explained that, as a mentor, Lennart never questioned the craft, you did things the way you were supposed to because: *that's the way it is,* as he used to say. I had the pleasure of visiting Knut's workshop outside of Gothenburg, where there was a lifetime's worth of wood-slöjd. To say I felt fortunate to get a first-hand look at his extensive body of work would be an understatement. Especially as he had been there, in person, on-site in Risa, for the documentation of Lennart becoming the Hedared basket's first 'last maker'. Knut handed me a stack of faded, handwritten notes. They dated back to the late 1970s and spanned across eleven pages. During the making of the documentary, he had recorded his observations of the material process. The notes were written with simple illustrations that demonstrate the procedures for obtaining the annual rings, from start to finish (even featuring Lennart's phone number from the time, written on their front page).

Fast-forward a few decades to when I worked with Curt in Risa: we skipped the most intricate and logistically complex parts of the Hedared basket's material process—felling a tree, and precisely cutting its log to the correct dimensions.

Yet, Curt was thorough in his descriptions. To illustrate the parts of the process we had bypassed, he made a series of simple drawings (accompanied by recorded instructions), similar to the ones Knut had drawn.

The same type of notes, made some forty years later.

***

It all comes back to the annual rings. Through Curt's skill, I held a piece of the local land, processed into a tangible link between Lennart and me, to our shared heritage. Obtaining the annual rings allowed me to experience the core elements of a traditional slöjd practice in action.

I wanted my work to be infused with this first-hand exposure to tradition, reflecting the unique capabilities of the

Virket för korgflätningen, tas av gran
och fur. Hälst kvistrena och rakvuxna
stammar 30% ø 1500 - 1800% långa. På
furen kan en bit bark tas av, så ser
man om fibrerna går rakt eller
lite till vänster   ) Furen skall
vara senvuxen (många årsringar.)
Gran kan inte barken tas av för då
ruttnar den, när den står på rot.) Den skall
barkas noga efter den är huggen annars går
barkborren inn. Granen kan vara snabbvuxen.
Granen skall gå rakt eller lite till höger.

Stockarna delas upp i 8 eller 16 delar
efter storlek. Och kärnveden huggs
bort, så ungefär 1/3 återstår.

stocken delas isär med kilar

278

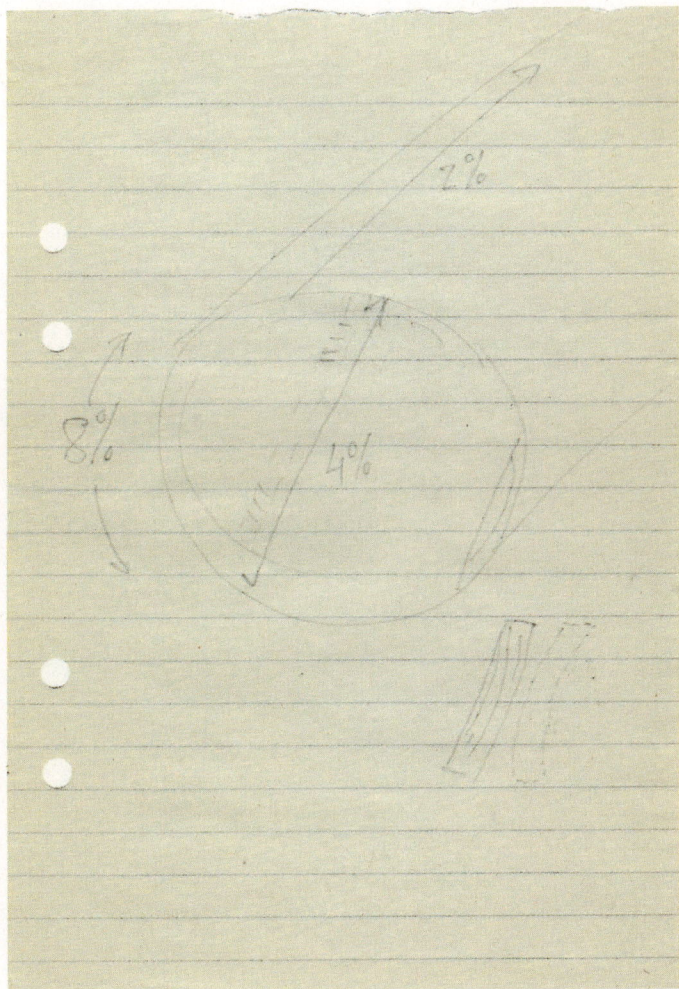

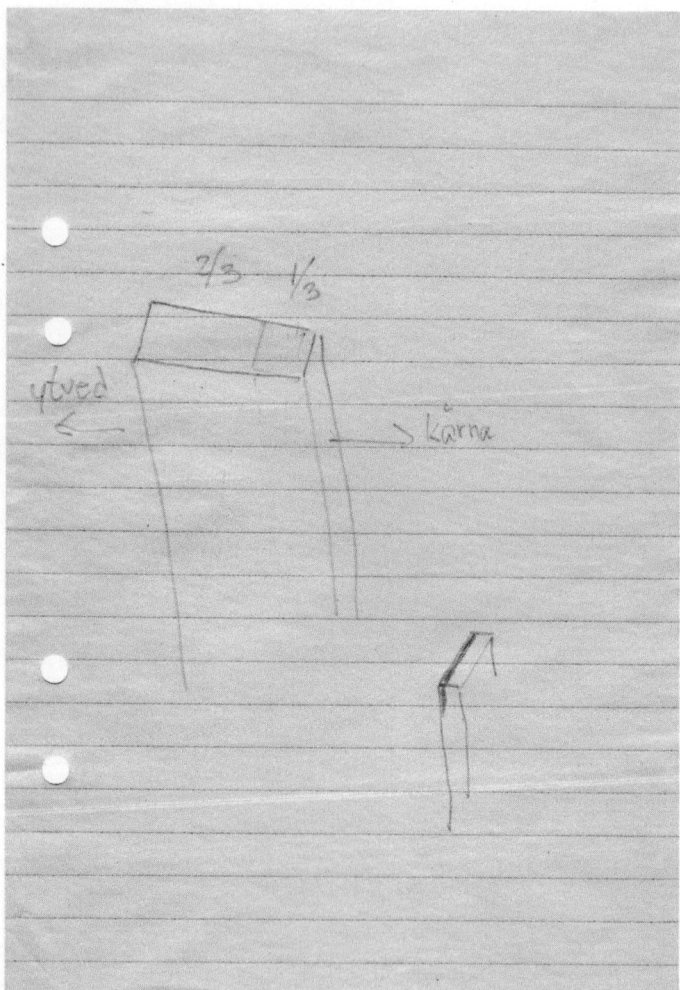

2/3 1/3

ytved

← kärna →

280

Hedared makers, both past and present. The annual rings gave the project's deeper sense of purpose material form. I wanted its sense of purpose to resonate with others, for outsiders to grasp its many layers and complexities. Their tactile nature helps retell their own story.

Hearing about a rural craft tradition centred around making utilitarian objects from the insides of pine trees can undoubtedly seem too abstract to comprehend (perhaps even for the most experienced of wood-slöjdare).

Seeing, however, is believing.

I not only cherish these rings, they are among my most prized possessions. Through them, I carry Lennart with me while holding the story of our family in my hands.

***

Curt stressed that the knowledge of the basket belonged not to him alone but to the village. He described how Gustav Persson had 'given' him his skills, and now, as the primary owner of the knowledge, he saw it as his task to continue passing it on, for its tradition to live beyond him. Like Gustav, as keeper of the basket's knowledge in the twenty-first century, Curt has agency—the freedom to infuse himself into *his* making.

If we first look at the objects made by Lennart and use them as the epitome of traditional aesthetics, a sort of generalised visual default for the Hedared basket, the common denominator across the different objects he made is that they a) look like a basket, b) have a utilitarian purpose. Whether more intricate or simple in style, the basket is a basket.

Cut to Gustav. He rediscovered the craft after retiring. In his later years, Persson made baskets out of pure lust, which bred a freedom that allowed a playful examination of its form and function. From slightly altering the rounded proportions of the traditional förnings basket (making its shape more oval), to making miniature replicas, or 'basketing' what resembled toy cars—Gustav freely, and continuously, explored new avenues across a spectrum of wood-slöjd.

GUSTAV

Finally, in the case of Curt (the former student of Gustav), a play with colour and material has been introduced: most notably in the use of colourful knitted textiles in the handle of the traditional berry-picking basket. Gustav was, and Curt still is, open to shaping the familiar material of the basket into new and personal formations. Gustav understood the traditional methods of the past but wasn't confined by them. Similarly to Curt, that kind of explorative approach to making has allowed their objects to become vessels of self-expression.

For a basket to be a *Hedared* basket, it must be made with the annual rings from senvuxen pine, derived through its unique processes. Its appearance and use are secondary to the material, as its form and function are simply a reflection of each artisan. A Hedared basket may, therefore, be adorned with colourful knits or shaped like a toy car, but through its material, it remains a Hedared basket.

As Curt puts it: *the material is its soul.*

***

Early on, I knew I wouldn't make an actual basket, my interest and expertise lie elsewhere. I make two-dimensional cloth, not three-dimensional wooden structures. Much like Gustav and Curt, I, too, don't want to revere tradition as sacred to the point where it can't find new and other contexts to exist within. While I have reverence for Lennart and his lived reality, it was not the re-enactment of historical processes I sought to find in *my* slöjd.

I wanted to explore how the methodology behind the Hedared basket could be translated into my own medium, as an extension of my core interest: to communicate the cultural evolution that has occurred in our family. I wanted to take the basket out of the idealistic framework of traditional slöjd and bring it into my own, seemingly freer, realm of making—where the written word helps to aid the comprehension of its new context. I wanted my perspective on allmoge to be about being in keeping with the past (with tradition), but for it to be firmly situated in the present. As described, when growing up, I was predominately culturally versed in a Western, heteronormative context with Swedish as my first language—despite my shared Swedish and North African heritage. The inherent sense of in-betweenship created by these multiple points of view; being unable to speak Arabic whilst adhering to Eurocentric cultural norms, often led to friction within myself, in not being perceived to belong (or adhere) to one cultural context. The longing for acceptance and togetherness continues to make itself known, particularly through my inability to speak the language from which my own name originates.

Arabic is a familiar, intimate, yet foreign tongue.

Its absence has left an innate longing to be able to communicate my existence to the outside world (within this kaleidoscope of identities) and led me to seek outlets that would allow for self-expression beyond the spoken. Craft continues to be the liberating process from which I can find self-acceptance and comprehend my place in the world whilst communicating beyond barriers of language or culture. It is the outward manifestation of this ever-evolving, internal contemplation.

***

The conclusion of this text's original form, my then dissertation, reads:

> *I have used the Hedared basket: its past practitioners and its socio-geographically unique material process to inform and help steer my own making. In my studio-based work, the research itself has served as the subject, allowing the explored themes of place, cultural history, design, craft, belonging and identity to coalesce into one. The research became a platform for exploration and discovery. Together, the written research and my studio-based work allowed me to regard my mixed cultural heritage, belief in storytelling, craft practice and studies in design as tools in an arsenal from which to innovate and recontextualise.*

286

The rigid discipline and industriousness found in the material process of the Hedared basket prompted me to act in the same way: to build a self-sufficiency that would reflect my own context of being a handweaver in the twenty-first century. Applying my two-dimensional knowledge of working with woven textiles to the basket's three-dimensional landscape, I wished to celebrate the preciousness of the handmade in the context of the man-made. I decided to use CAD software and digital technologies such as 3D printing to approach the basket when recontextualising the rich craftsmanship of its material process.

Having presented plastic as an indicator for contemporary material culture, the idea of creating a synergy between myself as a maker and a chosen material became a prominent feature, as was the case with my great-grandfather Lennart and his primary use of pine. The research led me to use biodegradable PLA plastic pellets together with pine fibres taken from scraps of the annual tree rings, to develop a biodegradable wooden filament yarn: a 'Hedared filament'.

By using automated machinery, the traditional directness of the hand is mediated through the industrial equipment used. I celebrate the handicraft behind the Hedared basket through the application of modern-day technology. The added dimension of, not only mind, hand and heart, but an emphasis on the connection between maker and machine, adds a new layer of process. The union between plastic and pine, the past and the present—between me and Lennart—summarises the research conducted thus far, and manifests in the physical material produced. The values of tradition merge in the present through the elusive properties of the synthetic.

I connect the making of the basket to the ability to effortlessly navigate both known and unspoken cultural cues: adhering to the unwavering ways of Västgötska. Historically, the makers in Risa reflected a lack of social prominence.

Today, the basket is a great source of pride. Hedared's basketry tradition is a celebrated and nationally revered cultural heritage. A tree needed for the raw material of the basket is older than Hulta as we know it today. Much like the plastic artefacts found in Borås Museum of History's archive, Hulta's monumental landscape appears everlasting but carries a sense of transience.

I wanted to materialise the many aspects of Hulta: its conception, environment, energy, and the often hard-to-grasp lived experiences of its inhabitants. I wished for these aspects to become equally as tangible as the histories held in the annual rings. For me, the filament material represents the emergence of a process that not only embodies the lived experience of the parts involved in the research but intersects with the discoveries and exploration of making the material itself—an ever-embracing process of trial and error. I wished for it to hold the patchwork of approaches and perspectives that this project has been as a whole: a non-linear process, not in need of a final form, but rather a tangible body, to host these various notions.

***

I continued in the conclusion of this text's original form, my then dissertation, to say:

> *During the process of writing this text, I had to analyse the connections between myself, my practice and the greater world around me. I have discovered the universally spoken language of craft: its transformative potential and its many intricacies. Anchoring these bodies of text as part of my final undergraduate project, having studied on a practical, hands-on design course, this written*

research has presented a new way of approaching and comprehending my work. The research process has presented how theory can inform a making-based practice and vice versa. It has opened up new perspectives and connected my own ethos with that of already established and globally relevant ideas on craft.

***

Whilst I am vastly separated from the living conditions of my great-grandfather, growing up with multiple cultural references as a queer person in a working-class environment, the recurrent need to conform, find meaning and belonging has continued to colour my desire to make. When seeking to deconstruct the cultural evolution and detangle the web of intricacies between me and Lennart, necessity becomes a key link—to get by and to find the tools to facilitate this need—by using craft.

As the outward manifestation of this ever-evolving, internal contemplation, craft continues to be the process through which I navigate my multitude of identities, a process that continuously seeks to reflect the creation of a space in which to exist and belong.

IMAGE CREDITS

Unless specified, all images were either taken by the author in 2020 or sourced from the author's personal photo albums. In the latter case, the dates and the photographer's identity are unknown.

p. 278:
Note, Knut Östgård (n.d.).
pp. 279–280:
Notes, Curt Bengtsson (2020).
p. 282:
Film still: Jansson, I. (1978) *Slöjd från Sjuhärad: Korgslöjd i Hedared*. Borås: De sju häradernas hemslöjdsförening/Slöjd i Väst/Kulturförvaltningen VGR.
p. 284:
Images courtesy of Curt Bengtsson (n.d.).
pp. 291–292:
Process: jacquard woven cloth (2020).
pp. 292–293:
An Ode to Lennart (white on white) (2020). Photo: Molly Overstall Khan.
pp. 294–297:
Process: jacquard woven cloths (2020).
pp. 298–301:
Process: material development (2021). Photo: Molly Overstall Khan.
pp. 302–303:
Process: 3D printed imagery and jacquard woven cloths (2020). Photo: Molly Overstall Khan.
p. 304:
An Ode to Lennart (white on white) (2020). Photo: Molly Overstall Khan.
p. 305:
An Ode to Lennart (2021). Photo: Molly Overstall Khan.
pp. 306–311:
Weaving in progress (2023). Photo: Molly Overstall Khan.
pp. 312–313:
In Thoughts, *Together* (2023). Photo: Alexis Rodríguez Cancino.
pp. 314–315:
Profanities (close-up) (2023).
p. 320:
Portrait (2023). Photo: Alexis Rodríguez Cancino.

294

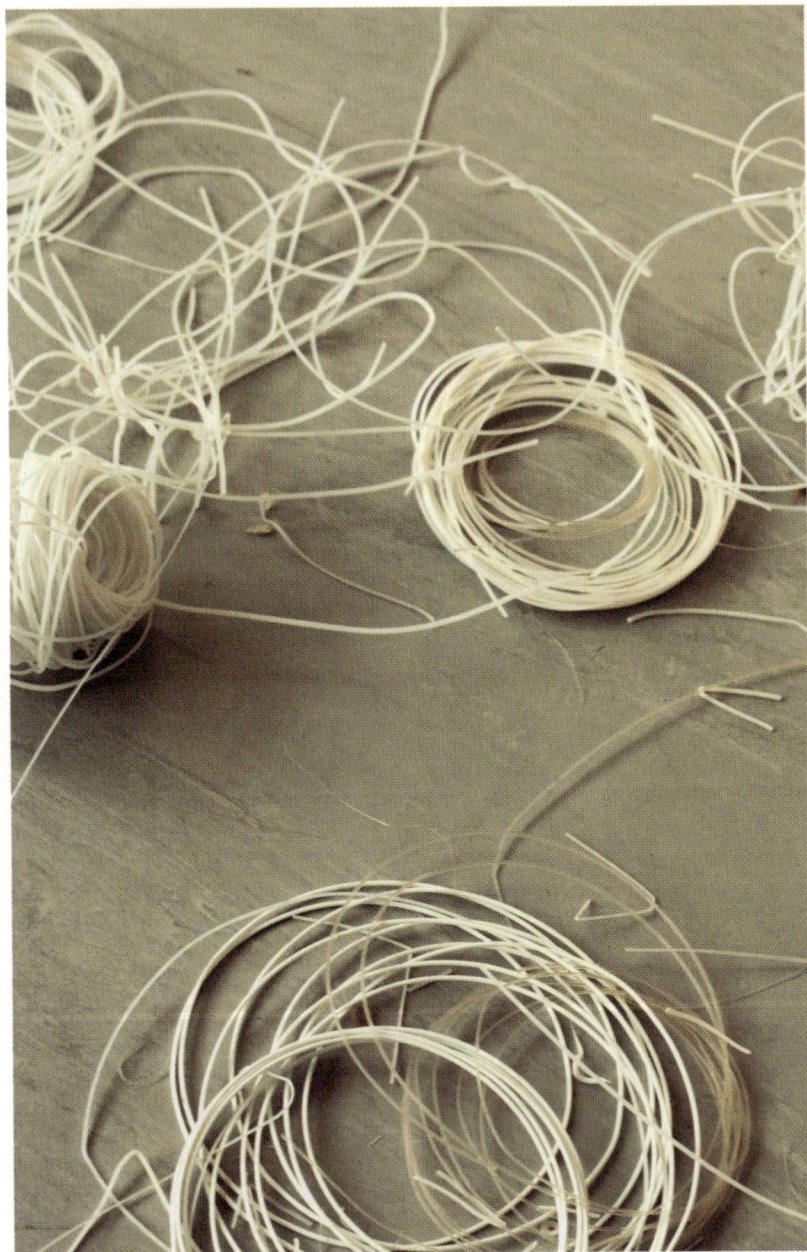

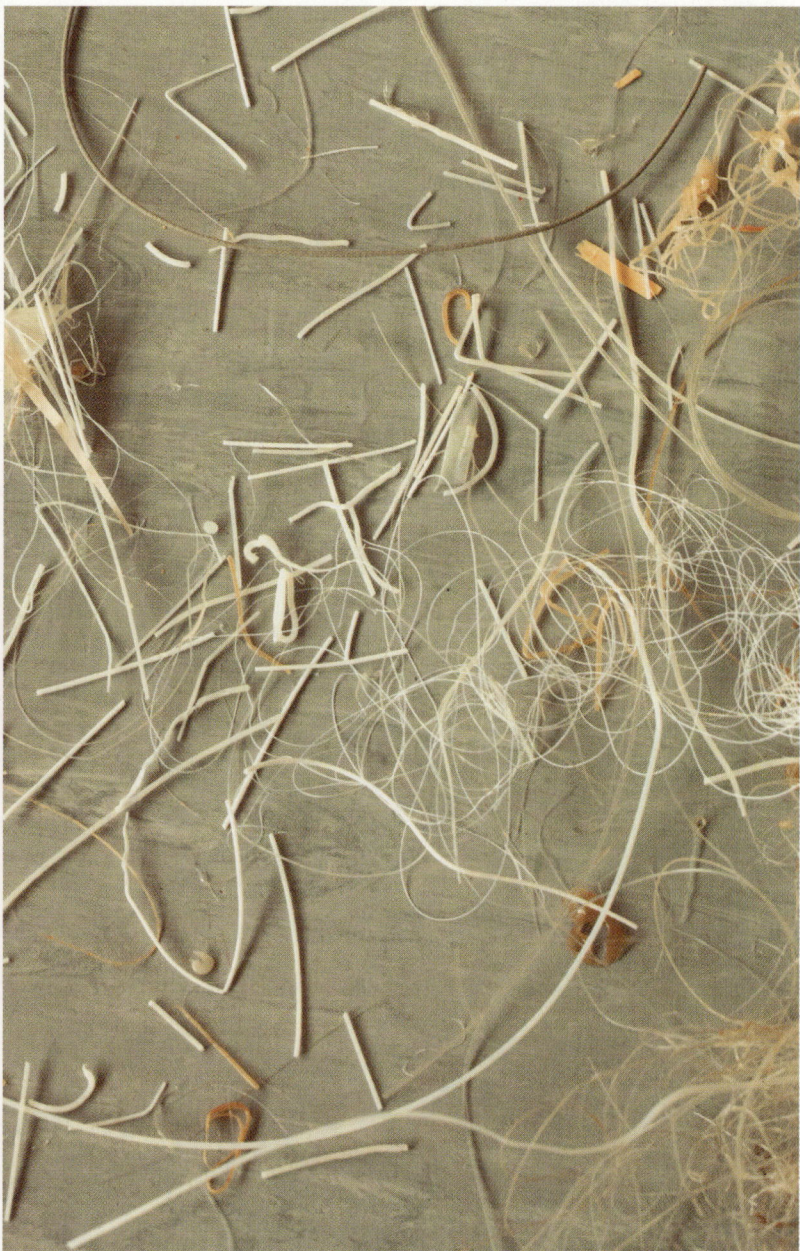

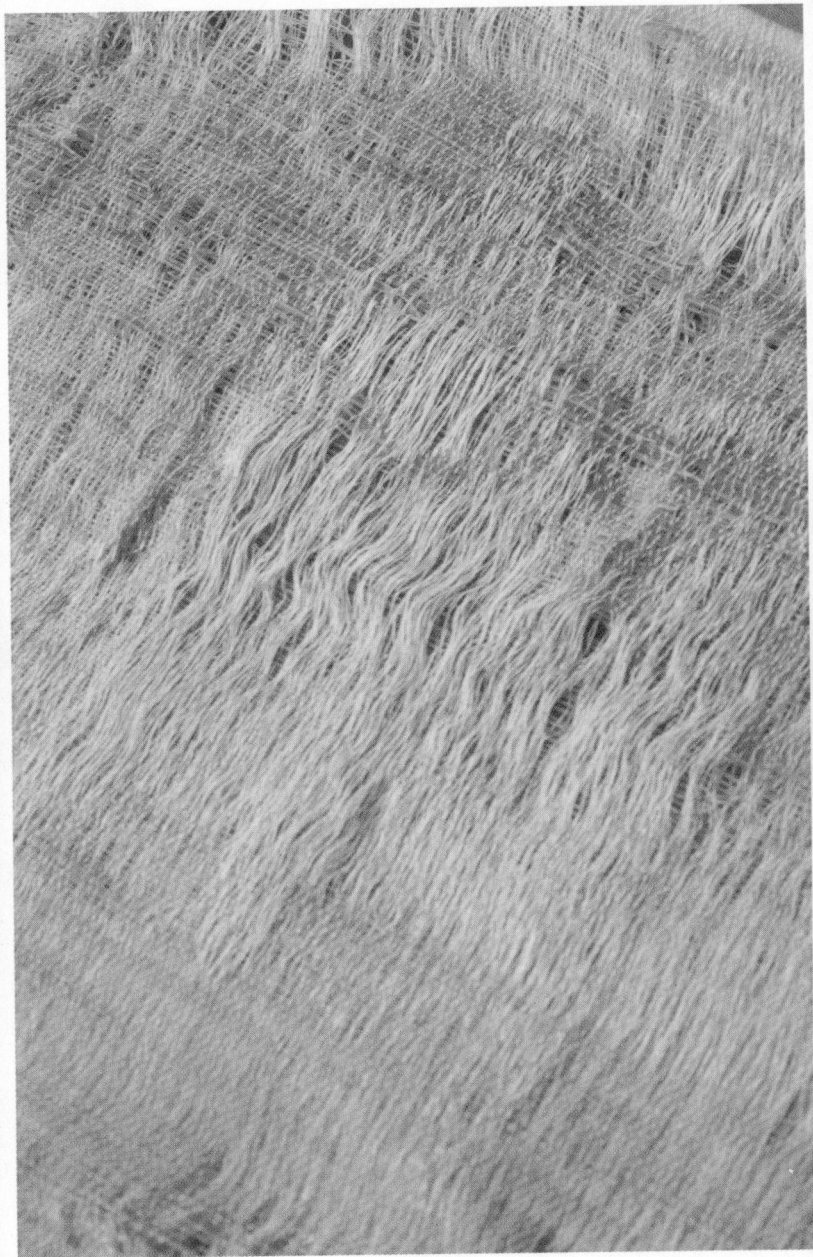

310

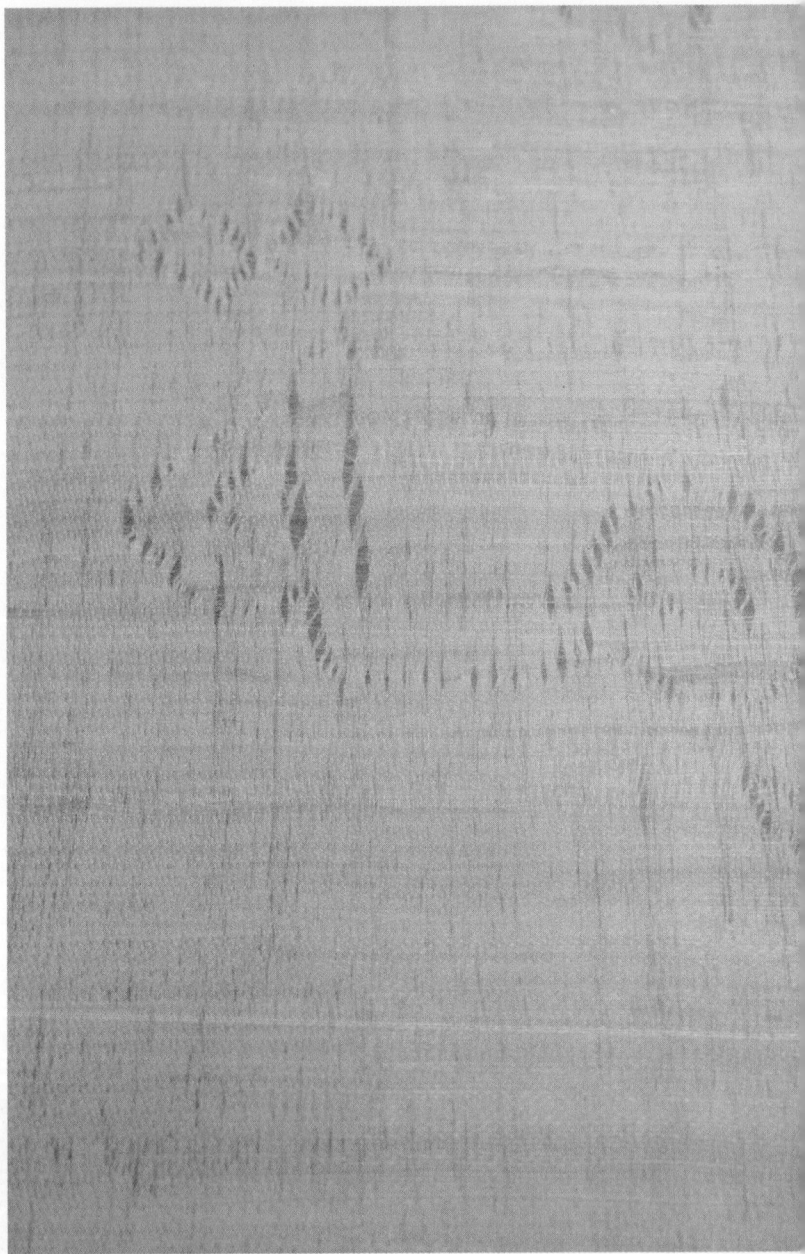

THANK YOU

Completing this book has been a long journey—one that would not have been possible without the dedication, generosity, and encouragement from so many people. Whether as direct contributors, collaborators, mentors, friends, or family, each has played a crucial role in bringing this project to life.

I am grateful to have had my family and friends believing in the long journey of bringing this book to life. I carry you all with me.

I am grateful to all the institutions and organisations who have supported, enriched, and lifted this project—Thank you.

In Sweden, we say *ingen nämnd, ingen glömd* (no one named, no one forgotten), yet credit where credit is due.

First and foremost, my deepest gratitude and most heartfelt thanks to Ulla Pettersson and Curt Bengtsson, without you, this project would not have been possible.

Ulla, for your continuous inspiration and wholehearted commitment. I am your biggest fan.

Curt, for your endless generosity, how will I ever repay your kindness?

Mary Restieaux, for your insightful guidance and unwavering support. I am forever grateful.

Sara Degerfält and Catarina Ingemarsson, for sharing your vast knowledge

Martha Cruz, for your critical eye

Hedareds byalag, for sharing their stories

Raisa Kabir, Tanya Harrod, Helena Hansson and Marcia Harvey Isaksson, for enriching this publication so immensely

Rynee Zhang, for your dedication

Lisa Olausson, for bringing the project visuals to life

Freek Lomme, for taking on the project

and to Lennart—for opening up the whole world

With all my gratitude,
Fadhel

COLOPHON

Set Margins' #23
The ~~Last Basket~~ Makers from Risa:
Crafting a Plural Kinship along Tradition

ISBN: 978-90-834993-0-7

Author: Fadhel Mourali
Contributing Authors: Raisa Kabir,
Tanya Harrod, Helena Hansson,
Marcia Harvey Isaksson
Graphic Designer: Lisa Olausson
Graphic Assistant: Rynee Zhang,
Chao-chi Lau
Text Editor: Martha Cruz
Proofreader: Kesara Ariya
Photographers: Molly Overstall
Khan, Alexis Cancino Rodríguez
Project Advisor: Freek Lomme

Printer: Printon, Tallin (Est.)
Papers: Rives Shetland Bright
White 250g/m², Holmen BOOK
70g/m²
Fonts: Ivar Text, Monument
Grotesk

This publication is made possible
thanks to the generous support
of Tore G. Wärenstams Stiftelse,
HEDA Sand & Betong,
Älvsborgs Läns Hemslöjdsförbund,
Stiftelsen Längmanska
Kulturfonden, by my own
investment and the contribution of
my family.

Research was graciously supported
by The National Swedish
Handicraft Council.

Tore G Wärenstams stiftelse

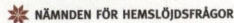

HEDA

Hemslöjden

STIFTELSEN
**LÄNGMANSKA
KULTURFONDEN**
GRUNDAD 1859

NÄMNDEN FÖR HEMSLÖJDSFRÅGOR

First edition, 2025

Set Margins'
www.setmargins.press

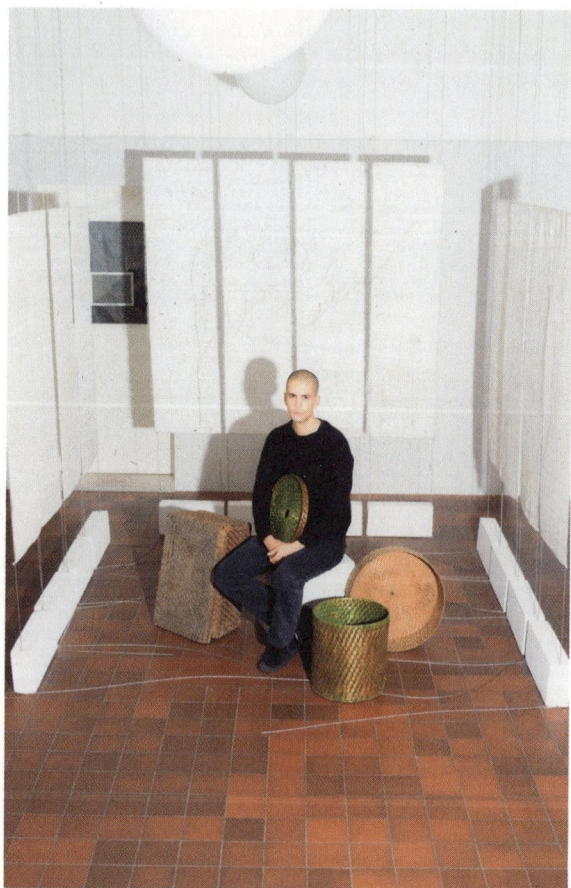